I0901705

REMEMBERING CHELTENHAM TOWNSHIP

DONALD SCOTT SR.

THE History PRESS

Published by The History Press
Charleston, SC 29403
www.historypress.net

First published 2009

Manufactured in the United States

ISBN 978.1.59629.749.4

Library of Congress Cataloging-in-Publication Data

Scott, Donald, 1954-
Remembering Cheltenham Township / Donald Scott, Sr.
p. cm.
Includes bibliographical references.
ISBN 978-1-59629-749-4
1. Cheltenham (Pa. : Township)--History. 2. Cheltenham (Pa. : Township)--Biography.
I. Title.
F159.C49S38 2009
974.8'12--dc22
2009041743

Dedicated to my extraordinary mother, Mrs. Grace Scott, as well as bygone heavenly friends and history connoisseurs Philip Kind and Arnold Snyder, who both encouraged me to write this book.

CONTENTS

ACKNOWLEDGEMENTS

Remembering Cheltenham Township was made possible by the many valued documents, manuscripts, images, photographs and portraits generously provided to the author by numerous community organizations, institutes, agencies and historical societies, among them Cheltenham Township Historical Commission; Cheltenham Township School District: Old York Road Historical Society; Historical Society of Montgomery County (Pennsylvania); Historical Society of Pennsylvania; Pennsylvania Museum and Historical Commission; Richard Wall House Museum; Citizens for the Restoration of Historic LaMott (CROHL); St. Paul's Episcopal Church of Elkins Park; and the Philadelphia Museum of Art.

Additional information used to complete this project was supplied by the Pennsylvania State Archives, U.S. Army Military History Institute, Library of Congress, Union League of Philadelphia, Free Library of Philadelphia, Library Company of Philadelphia, Friends Historical Library at Swarthmore College and the Jenkintown Library.

The author wishes to express his deepest gratitude and appreciation to township officials, colleagues, friends and family for sharing their talent, expertise and resources, including Bill Chambrés, Leon Clemmer, Thomas I. Dawson, Nancy Gibson, James Elton Johnson, Elizabeth Cataldi, Charis Bowling, Lise Marlowe, James M. Paradis, William Pickens III, David B. Rowland, Donald Scott Jr., Kristopher Scott, Dorothy Spruill, Norman

Triplett, Jack and Mary Washington and Joyce Werkman. Finally, the author wishes to thank his wife, Billie, and father-in-law, Wesley A. Brown, for their immense support and encouragement; thanks also to the superb residents of Cheltenham Township, past and present, for their inspiration.

INTRODUCTION

The diverse Pennsylvania countryside of woodland, rolling hills, meadows and streams in what would become eastern Montgomery County's Cheltenham Township was first utilized and honored by the Delaware (Leni-Lenape) natives, or "original people," of the area for several thousand years. That was before Englishmen Richard Wall and Toby Leech settled here in 1682, naming the area after their quaint hometown in Gloucestershire, England, that rose on the banks of the River Chelt likely following the establishment there of an ancient monastery in the year AD 803.

"Cheltenham might have derived its name from this monastery; as it was situated on one of the elevated spots near the town," wrote Thomas Frognall Dibdin and H. Ruff in their 1803 book, *The History of Cheltenham, and Account of its Environs*. "Thus the word Chilt and Ham, as originally signifying an elevated place, and monastery or village, may be the true foundation of the present word 'Cheltenham.'" The word "Cheltenham" could also be derived from "Cheltenhomme," meaning "the town under the hill," as other historical sources indicate.

The original English town, that today is an important cultural and historic "twin" of its American counterpart, became renowned over the centuries for upscale living, mineral water spas, horse racing, shopping and splendid fairs.

In Pennsylvania's eastern Montgomery County, a good portion of Cheltenham Township was home to the upper echelons of Philadelphia

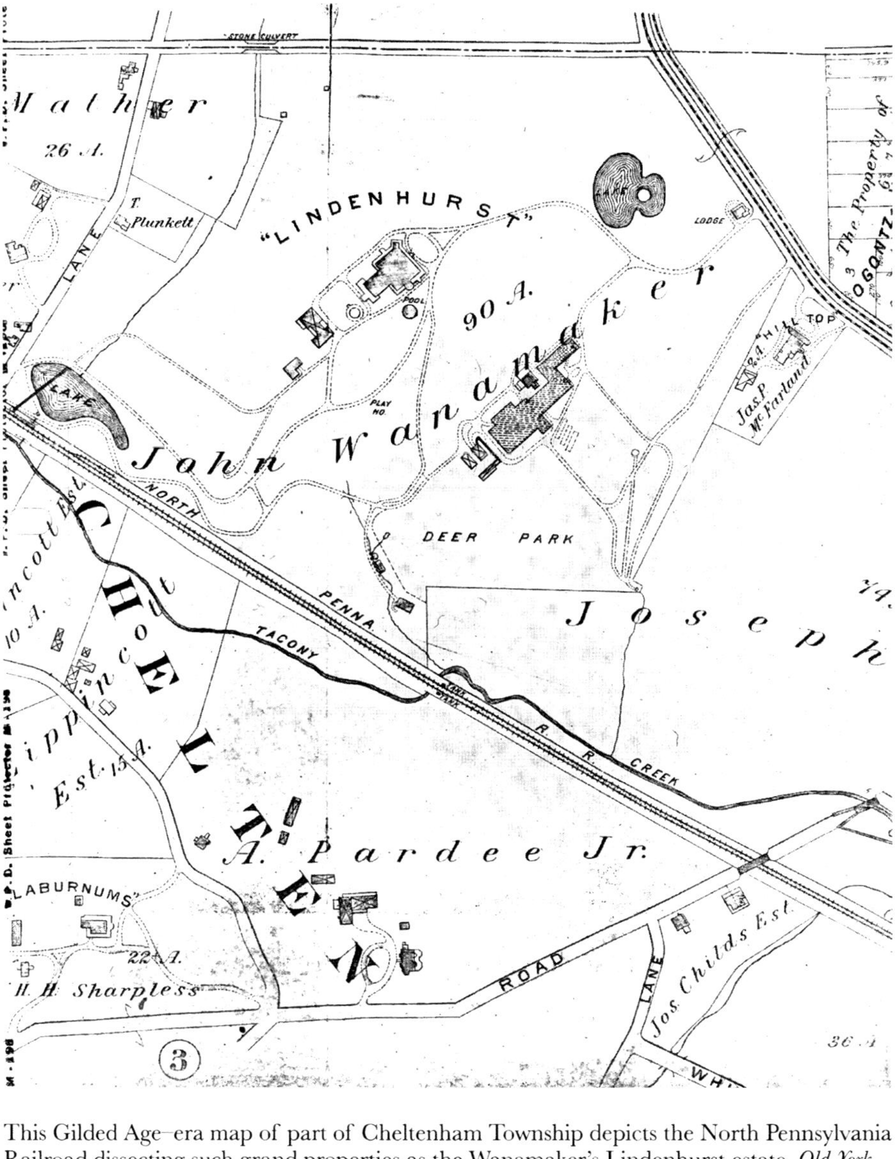

This Gilded Age–era map of part of Cheltenham Township depicts the North Pennsylvania Railroad dissecting such grand properties as the Wanamaker's Lindenhurst estate. *Old York Road Historical Society.*

society. Wealthy residents included investment banker Jay Cooke ("financier of the Civil War" for the Union) and such enterprising Gilded Age tycoons as ice cream maker Henry Breyer, department store magnate John Wanamaker, hat maker John Stetson, as well as transportation tycoon partners William Elkins and Peter A.B. Widener, whose family members were on the great ship *Titanic* as it sank to the North Atlantic's ocean floor in 1912. Some of America's most affluent and influential people still make Cheltenham home, including the mega entertainer and educator William "Bill" Cosby.

Yet locally, many of Cheltenham's first residents were Quakers who brought a religious zeal and civil rights principles that attracted to the area the greatest antislavery abolitionists in American history, who locally helped to establish the first and largest federal facility to train black Civil War soldiers, Camp William Penn; the hardworking Irish who labored in some of the first mills on the continent along the Tookany waterway; African Americans in search of "the Promised Land"; Jewish immigrants, responsible for developing legendary religious institutions and places of higher learning, producing the likes of Israel's Prime Minister Benjamin Netanyahu; and in more modern times, a nationally recognized Korean community, as well as West African immigrants.

The ninth-century monarch King Alfred the Great referred to Leech and Wall's hometown in England as very peaceful, noting its idyllic setting about ten miles east of Gloucester where the River Chelt emerges from the western Costwolds. Characterized by a range of ancient limestone hills, the Costwolds since 3000 BC were dotted with charming villages of hearty people who historically raised sheep.

Indeed, *this* American land—located across an almost endless ocean where Leech and Wall settled after what was an arduous journey in fragile European-built ships—had undulating hills that were full of game, lush trees and other resources important to the Native Americans for millennia.

The arrival of Leech and Wall would soon lead to the creation of one of the most historic communities in the region, if not the nation.

PART I

EARLY INHABITANTS, THEIR INDUSTRY AND REVOLUTIONARY WAR

Leni-Lenape and Chief Tamany

Home to the Leni-Lenape for thousands of years was the land that would be called Cheltenham, graced by gentle hills, thick forests and waterways, described by some explorers as having soaring flocks of birds so thick that they'd blot out the sun and schools of fish so plentiful that quiet waters seemed to be boiling as they swam by. The earth was worshipped and honored.

"Prior to the coming of [the state's founder] William Penn in 1682, Cheltenham Township was the hunting ground of the Lenni Lenape Indians, whose headquarters were on a bluff, overlooking the Neshaminy, near Newtown, Pennsylvania," which is today in nearby Bucks County, noted historian Ralph Morgan in his 1945 article, "Preserving the Heritage of Cheltenham Township," for the *Old York Road Historical Society Bulletin*.

Recognized by Europeans as the Delaware tribe, the Leni-Lenape inhabited southeastern Pennsylvania where Wall, Leech and the Quaker leader (the state's founder) William Penn made home searching for political autonomy, religious freedom and land. Penn, born in October 1644 in London, England, was a persecuted Quaker who was granted land by King Charles II due to a debt owed to his father, Admiral Sir William Penn. Young Penn named the new land "Pennsylvania," meaning "Penn's woods," for his

Today, the park system and paths along the creek are used by joggers and for recreational use. *Kristopher Scott.*

esteemed parent, a noted naval commander responsible for obtaining the island of Jamaica for the Crown.

More Quakers from England, Holland, Germany and Scandinavia, and other Protestants, from commoners to the affluent, soon followed Penn. The Cheltenham area, just northwest of Philadelphia, was attractive to them due to its enriched soil for farms and swift-running waterways that could power mills. "Tacony Creek was so called by the Indians, or as they called it, Tookany (meaning Heavily Wooded Stream)," according to Morgan.

Cheltenham, according to Morgan, was derived from "lands of Pennsylvania" that "were bestowed upon William Penn in 1681 by Charles the Second of England" when "Penn had plans drawn in England, and it is a significant fact that the boundaries conceived by his draftsmen in London in 1681, with very minor adjustment in the two hundred and sixty-three intervening years, are the identical boundaries of Cheltenham Township today." The township is located ten miles north of central Philadelphia and has an area of nine square miles.

Bean's 1884 History of Montgomery County, Pennsylvania, by Theodore Bean, notes the "earliest purchase by Penn of any part of what now constitutes Montgomery County was made the 25th of June, 1683, of [the Native American] Wingebone, for all his rights to lands lying on the west side of the

Schuylkill [River], beginning at the lower falls of the same, and so on up and backward of said stream as far as right goes." Cheltenham, in fact, is likely the earliest township given a name within Montgomery County, according to Bean.

A 1683 purchase by local Native American leaders Neneshickan, Malebore, Neshanocke and Oscreneon was made for the land between the Schuylkill and what is today Pennypacker Creek extending northwest to Conshohocken, likely including what is today Cheltenham and the surrounding areas.

Finally, the great Native American chief Tamany, with other local Indian leaders, sold a massive amount of land on July 5, 1697, between the Pennypacker and Neshaminy Creeks that started in Delaware and extending to "as far as a horse could travel in two days," according to Bean. This was the last of the land sold in Montgomery County by Native Americans, meaning according to the European purchasers they had no further rights to the land.

The land was considered exceptionally prime if it included a stream or river powerful enough to propel mills, similar to Cheltenham's terrain, which was crisscrossed by several of such coveted waterways.

Some nearby early watercourses were wide and deep enough to be navigated by European vessels, including those of the Swedish, who sailed up the nearby Pennypack as early as the mid-1600s. The name "Pennypack" was an Indian word that could be found as a variation on a Swedish map dating back to 1654.

Meanwhile, Tamany (or Tammany), a primary Delaware chief, was hailed by William Penn "as one of the finest characters" who the state's founder had met, likely due to prolifically "selling" land to the new settlers. The chief was also known by his people as Tamanend, meaning "the affable," for his pleasant personality. "He is noteworthy chiefly for the legends that have grown up around his name, perhaps arising from the fact that his was the first sale negotiated by William Penn personally," wrote Paul A.W. Wallace in *Indians in Pennsylvania*, published 1999.

Called Tammany by the English, he "has been portrayed as chief of all the Delaware Indians who met Penn in a legendary 'Great Treaty' held under the 'Treaty Elm' at Shakamaxon," and is depicted in the epic painting of the great colonial painter Benjamin West. A few sources speculate that Leech and Wall appeared with Penn at the meeting under the great elm. The legacy of Tamanend was so highly esteemed that a variety of European-American secret societies and quasi-political groups were named for the great indigenous American locally and well beyond southeastern Pennsylvania.

In Cheltenham, the Order of Red Men, a social and fraternal organization, was based on Rowland Avenue in a home originally built by Thomas Rowland for his daughter, Mary, and her husband, Frank Hansell. Almost two dozen bedrooms were added in 1914 with about four hundred men living at the facility over the years, according to the Old York Road Historical Society. The structure was demolished in 1964 when just four residents resided there.

Chief Tamanend's ancestors had been in Pennsylvania well before the birth of Christ. Native Americans were cultivating the ground "[m]ore than three thousand years ago in Pennsylvania," Wallace noted, adding that they grew corn or maize, known as "the mother of civilization in America." Indeed, the Delawares and other indigenous Americans passed on the techniques to cultivate such crops to local Europeans, which helped them to thrive and paradoxically take over the Native American land.

NATIVES' APPEARANCE, CUSTOMS

By the time Europeans began to arrive in Pennsylvania, the natives generally lived in harmony, except during relatively rare episodes of war. And their artistry, including the carving of ornaments from wood, animal bone and other products of nature, was exceptional. Such creativity extended to ceremonial clothing, as well as to dancing and singing usually linked to religious ceremonies based on the belief of a primary god and various spirits. Their social systems, although foreign to the Europeans, were overall nonviolent and had a variety of restraints or checks and balances as they lived gentle and harmonious lives.

The Delawares were an open amalgamation of Algonkian bands as the seventeenth century began, occupying land from the Delaware Bay to the Blue (or Kittatiny) Mountain and from the Atlantic coast to the Susquehanna watershed in Delaware. Their name—Delawares—was derived from the great river named for the Baron de la Warr, the first governor of Virginia. Europeans, either unacquainted with tribal identities or opting to generalize, referred to the area's natives as the "Delawares," even if they lived far beyond the Delaware River, Wallace observed.

William Penn, a contemporary of Cheltenham's original European settlers Leech and Wall, described in 1683 the Delawares in a letter to the "Free Society of Traders," as "generally tall, straight, well-built, and of singular Proportion; they thread strong and clever, and mostly walk with a lofty Chin: Of Complexion, Black, but by design, as the Gypsies of England: They grease themselves with Bears-fat clarified, and using no defence against Sun or Weather, their skins must needs be swarthy," according to Wallace's book. It is very likely that early Cheltenham settlers, including Wall and Leech, made similar observations.

Indeed, Wallace's physical descriptions of Native American men, who undoubtedly lived with their families and hunted in the Cheltenham area, are exceptionally detailed: "They had broad cheekbones and well-shaped but usually not prominent noses…differing from the hawk-nosed Indians of the Plains…Their eyes were dark. Their hair was black and straight. Like the gypsies, they were brown-skinned."

Their clothing reflected humble living in a woodland environment full of bountiful creatures. "The men wore a belt, a breachclout (equivalent to our bathing trunks), and moccasins—in summer as a rule, nothing more. Small children wore nothing at all," Wallace noted.

Natives Forced from Land

The local Leni-Lenape maintained a legendary respect for the land, even as they were forced out by shaky land deals and treaties that often required them to hunt many animal species to near local extinction in order to trade with settlers. This, then, according to Wallace, required them to move farther west as European settlers, including Quakers, placed more pressure on them—even those who lived in what became Cheltenham.

Although William Penn and local Quakers, compared to Europeans in other parts of the country, were kinder to the natives and even sometimes initially set aside land for them, the groundswell of immigrants over time almost completely led to the Indians' displacement in southeastern Pennsylvania and in Cheltenham.

The natives simply thought that they had made temporary agreements by trading land for goods since they conceived that no human being was capable of actually possessing the earth that really belonged to the creator.

They believed that the creator had endowed all humans with the right to honorably use the land and to share with one another as they traveled the countryside hunting and cultivating a limited number of crops.

It's clear today that the major thoroughfare in the township—Old York Road—was at one time a native path that led to hunting and fishing sources, similar to many of the major arteries in the Philadelphia metro area and other U.S. metropolises. Built in 1711, York Road actually was originally an Indian path that allowed the Leni-Lenape to travel to and from northern and southern locations that extended as far north as today's New York City. In the south, the road, becoming Broad Street, dissects Philadelphia as its primary street and leads to the Delaware River.

As the road systems developed, the English were generally aggressive, even if sometimes congenial, and scheming as they acquired native land. It's evident that Penn often bought the land using items of little European worth, including simple trinkets.

Even after Penn's death while a debtor in 1718, when his sons John, Richard and Thomas assumed the colony's proprietorship, many land violations against the natives continued. The brothers fell into debt, similar to their father, and began selling land to Europeans without first purchasing it from the Native Americans, as a variety of historical sources indicate.

The Penn brothers were not alone with respect to such infringements. Provincial Secretary James Logan, Pennsylvania's most significant administrator, also sold land to European settlers that actually belonged to the Indians. He was so prolific that many considered him to be a land speculator. For instance, Logan rigged up the "Walking Purchase" deal of 1737 with the natives to purchase land that would be measured by the distance of how far several men could walk from southeastern Pennsylvania toward the western part of the state. Several ploys and tricks, which included instigating friction between local tribes, were used to falsely extend the land claims, according to historians.

"William Penn's sons John and Thomas, as well as James Logan indicated clearly that they had abandoned William Penn's policy of fairness toward Native Americans. They seemed to have had no qualms about using one group of Indians to cheat another out of its land," noted an article published by the Pennsylvania State Archives, "The Walking Purchase: August 25, 1735."

The unfair practices of the Penns would come back to haunt Pennsylvania. Soon, the Delawares were forced west from their land but were welcomed by the French, who began fighting for territory in the Allegheny and Ohio River

Valley during the 1750s. The Delawares, according to the state archives, "moved down the Susquehanna and ravaged Pennsylvania's frontier. They destroyed crops, burned barns and homes, carried off and killed many of the colonists. The Quaker Party in the provincial legislature charged, probably validly, that the Delawares' actions were the direct result of the 'Walking Purchase.'"

Jay Cooke and Ogontz

Cheltenham, like many localities in southeastern Pennsylvania, would over the early years experience many associations with Native Americans, via the names of landmarks and other places, as well as by legend.

For instance, more than a century following the mid-1750s, the story would emerge of Chief Ogontz, who supposedly befriended a young boy in Ohio destined to make Cheltenham his home. That youngster, Jay Cooke, would also become the "financier of the Civil War" for Union forces and befriend the likes of President Abraham Lincoln and General Ulysses Grant, whose son would attend a local military academy that once sat where the Cheltenham School District's administration building is situated today. And

Jay Cooke's presence in Cheltenham would set the stage for the grand Gilded Age in Cheltenham, perhaps America's most acclaimed neighborhood in that regard. *Free Library of Philadelphia.*

Cooke would lead the way for Cheltenham's preeminence during the Gilded Age of the late 1800s and early 1900s.

In fact, on February 14, 1867, Cooke gave a "house warming" party at his lavish estate in Cheltenham, according to Lila Finck's 1984 article "The Legend of Ogontz" in the *Old York Road Historical Society Bulletin*. The guest list of five hundred included many dignitaries celebrating "the dedication of Mr. Cooke's new residence—an extravagantly decorated 52-room Victorian mansion that had taken nearly 18 months to build," Finck wrote. "At the celebration, Mr. Cooke christened his mansion Ogontz to honor the name and memory of a famous Ottawa Indian Chief the wealthy banker had admired and respected since childhood."

According to Finck, the Ogontz mansion was called "the showplace of the nation," erected in the midst of two hundred acres near "what is now Ashbourne Road, Church Road, and Washington Lane." She notes that Cooke's Ogontz was a grand estate at which he even entertained a U.S. president: "On the night of September 17, 1873, after a routine visit to Philadelphia, President Grant arrived at Ogontz, the palatial home of Jay Cooke. Ogontz had fifty-two rooms, including a conservatory and a full-scale theater. Its walls were decorated with frescoes. An Italian garden contained fountains and statuary. In the palace of honor in the main hall stood a statue of Ogontz, the Indian chief for whom this place was named." Yet the writer further notes: "No one remarked that the genocide of the Indians had made possible the fortune that built this edifice."

When "Cooke was in his mid-seventies, retired, and living in the Elkins Park residence of his son-in-law Mr. Charles D. Barney [who would co-found the firm Smith, Barney Co.]," Cooke wrote about Chief Ogontz:

> *At my birth in a town now called Sandusky, the place was frequently overrun with Indians. Old Ogontz did himself and us the honor of occasionally sojourning for a few days on the spot where he had once dwelt in his wigwam. On such occasions he was allowed to camp in our barn and my mother fed him bountifully at the kitchen table. I was his favorite and occasionally was mounted on his shoulders for a ride.*

Although Finck questions whether Cooke actually met Chief Ogontz, since the Native American probably "died in 1812, nine years before Jay Cooke was born," Penn State online historical information indicates that "Chief Ogontz taught Cooke wilderness skills as a boy and Cooke admired him greatly."

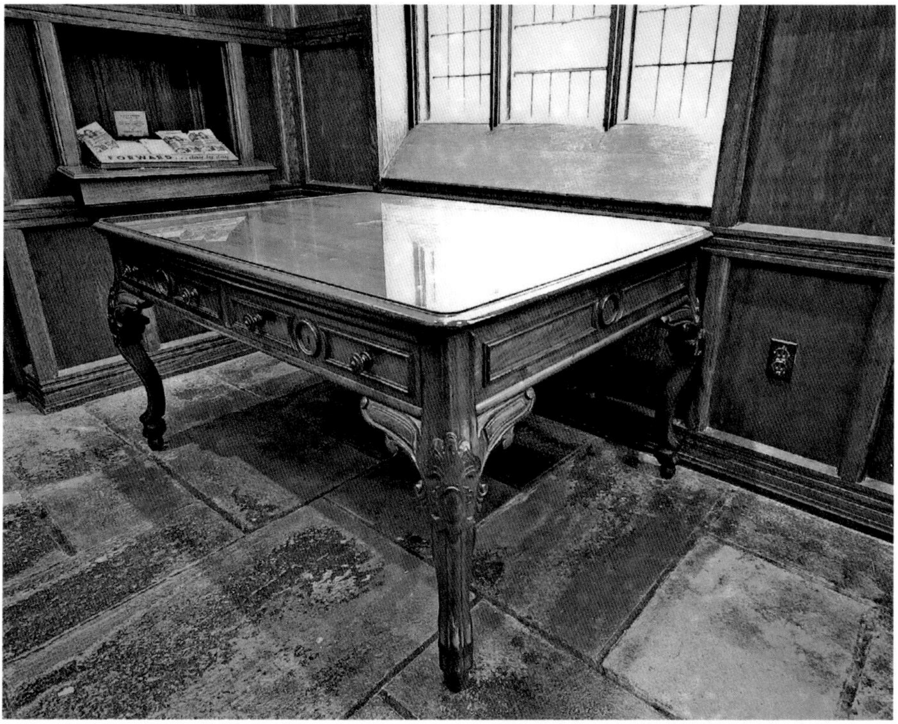

Above: Jay Cooke, the "financier of the Civil War" for Union forces, often used this desk for work, and it is on display at St. Paul's. *Kristopher Scott.*

Right: Jay Cooke was a close friend to President Ulysses Grant, whose son Jesse attended the Cheltenham Military Academy adjacent to Cooke's huge estate. *Free Library of Philadelphia.*

Yet there were certainly very tough times for the chief who was eventually killed by the son of a fellow tribal member whom Ogontz was forced to kill due to the Indian's envy (this was despite Ogontz adopting the murderous lad as dictated by Native American customs).

Today, the memory and name of Ogontz lives through the ages because it has been adopted by various entities in the area, including the Ogontz Fire Company of Elkins Park, a community previously known as Ogontz.

EARLY FOUNDERS, HOMESTEADS, CHURCHES, FARMS AND MILLS

Well before the formation of such establishments and grand estates as Ogontz in Cheltenham, early Europeans and blacks, who were sometimes used as slave labor by those settlers, established vital farms and mills that provided the foundation for future development. The gristmills were essential to manufacture grain to make bread for people and feed farm and domesticated animals such as horses.

The development of homesteads and mills cannot be separated from the founding of Cheltenham by Toby Leech and Richard Wall. Both men were involved with establishing early mills and homesteads in Cheltenham after they settled here in 1682.

There's tentative evidence indicating that Leech and Wall sailed with William Penn "in the Welcome 1682, landed at Upland, and were present at Penn's famous treaty with the Indians, but no written evidence of all this has ever been found," according to Horace Mather Lippincott's paper "Toby Leech" that he read to the Old York Road Historical Society on May 14, 1947.

However, Elaine W. Rothchild's 1976 book *A History of Cheltenham Township* indicates that Leech and his family arrived "onboard the Bristol Factor on October 28, 1682," around the time that the Welcome landed.

They were among Cheltenham's fifteen "First Purchasers," according to Rothschild, "who took advantage of Penn's offer to take part in his experiment in the New World." All were likely English Quakers, she noted.

One of those original purchasers of Cheltenham-area land, Humphrey Morrey, would become Philadelphia's first mayor in 1691, keeping in mind that areas such as Cheltenham were considered to be part of Philadelphia during the city's early history. Morrey's son Richard, who inherited the 250 acres that his father first purchased in 1683, would develop a relationship with one of the estate's slaves, Cremona, and have five children with her, leaving Cremona 198 acres upon his death. Richard Morrey earlier liberated Cremona and her children, making him one of the first Quakers to do so in early America.

Other "First Purchasers" who acquired Cheltenham land in 1682 and 1683 ranging from one hundred acres to five hundred acres included Thomas Phillips, Mary Mercy Jefferson, William Frampton, John Russell, Patrick Robinson, Richard Wall Jr., Richard Wall Sr., John Ashmead, Everard Bolton, William Brown, John Day, Nehemiah Mitchell and John West, notes Rothchild.

Yet it's undeniable that Leech and Wall founded what is today Cheltenham Township, as well as named it after they arrived in 1682, purchasing large tracts of land near each other. After all, both were members of Gloucester Monthly Meeting in England, whose members initially met at the home of Richard Wall.

Tobias Leech: The Country Gentleman

Leech certainly had impressive wealth. He also bought large amounts of land in Philadelphia along the Delaware River, much of it very prime due to its riverside locations.

In addition to purchasing land on Reedy Island in the Delaware River and in what is today New Castle County in Delaware, Leech bought 604 acres in Cheltenham Township adjacent to Richard Wall on August 9, 1706, via a transaction with William Penn. He constructed his home on what is today Church Road where it intersects Cedar Road, around a half-mile from the developing village of Shoemakertown, eventually to become Ogontz or Elkins Park today.

Leech, described as "an English country gentleman," established along the Tacony Creek a gristmill and tanning business, surely a sign of the abundant wildlife in the area. The slaves he owned undoubtedly helped him with his enterprises.

In his spare time, Leech reportedly hunted foxes in the English gentlemen's tradition, favoring an area not far from his home that became known as the Fox Chase area of Philadelphia.

Tookany Creek, originally known as Tacony, was the center of mill activity throughout the township's early history. *Kristopher Scott.*

Yet Leech and Wall were quite close even before sailing from England to these shores; Leech made his wedding vows in Wall's English abode. On October 26, 1679, Leech married Esther Ashmead, who was the daughter of John and Mary Ashmead, as historical documents indicate. The couple journeyed to Philadelphia 1682, bringing an infant son, Toby Jr., and the bride's mother, Mary Ashmead. Sadly, John Ashmead, Mary's husband, reportedly died during the trans-Atlantic voyage.

Once arriving in America, Leech and Wall helped to establish the Cheltenham Meeting that met in Richard Wall's house at Old York Road and Church Road in Elkins Park, where today Cheltenham Township has preserved the historic property as a museum. Several sources indicate that the structure, used as an early meetinghouse for the Quakers, is one of the oldest European-built houses in Pennsylvania and America that has been continually occupied. Leech, in fact, is a signed witness to marriages held at the property, including for Sarah Wall (the granddaughter of his friend Richard Wall) and George Shoemaker, whose family would establish a booming mill enterprise along the Tacony stream, today known as Tookany Creek.

Furthermore, members of that monthly meeting supported the first protest against slavery in 1688 in what is today the Germantown section of Philadelphia.

Yet Leech soon departed the Society of Friends to follow the outspoken Protestant George Keith in 1690 because later he is associated with the Church of England and former Quakers who established Trinity Church in Philadelphia. In fact, historians say that there's evidence that Trinity's history is directly tied to Quakerism.

Meanwhile, there's no doubt that Leech was very enterprising. "Toby Leech's various industries of milling, tanning, and baking were essentials in the new land, and made money for him," Lippincott asserted. "He baked sea-buisquit which he hauled to the city and sold to the shippers," as well as helped to build Old York Road.

Leech's children certainly benefited from his wealth and enterprise. His surviving children and their birth years included Toby (1680), John (1682) and Hester (1685), who married shipmaster and builder Bartholomew Penrose of a distinguished Philadelphia family. Two of his daughters, according to Lippincott, died as infants.

RICHARD WALL: A BUILDER OF RELIGIOUS SPIRIT AND HOPE

Earlier in 1682, Wall's family acquired through William Penn six hundred acres in Cheltenham after arriving in America during the summer of 1682 with his wife Joane Wheel and son Richard Wall Jr. and his wife, as well as Wall's granddaughter Sarah. He likely built a residence before winter set in, especially since there was substantial wood and stone in the area nearby. Dorothy Spruill, curator of the Richard Wall House Museum, believes the structure was possibly two stories and made of logs with a "stone end."

Nevertheless, the original building was likely very modest, consisting of a few rooms without a cellar. The structure was greatly expanded about 1725. The home (also known as the Ivy), today listed on the National Register of Historic Places, became the center of the blossoming community, serving as a meetinghouse for the Quakers.

That meetinghouse also gave birth to the Abington Meeting in nearby Abington Township in the 500 block of Meetinghouse Road near Greenwood Avenue between 1699 and 1702. In short, Richard Wall "was a concerned

The Wall House (also known as the Ivy) today is listed on the National Register of Historic Places. It became the center of the blossoming community, serving as a meetinghouse for the Quakers where many marriages were performed. *Old York Road Historical Society.*

Friend, a prominent and large land owner, and may be considered the founder of Abington Meeting of Friends," Lippincott contended.

Joined in marriage to the Shoemaker family, the Wall-Shoemaker clans owned the corn gristmill on the nearby Tacony Creek, while descendants of the Walls occupied the house until 1847, followed by the Boslers. The house was added to and/or redesigned in 1730, 1760 and 1805.

The Wall House since 1980 has been operated by the Cheltenham Township Historical Commission and serves as a museum featuring displays associated with the area's earliest times through post–World War II periods.

The Shoemakers Spark Early Mill Industry

The Shoemakers—with family roots according to Lippincott from Germany's Creshem or Kriegshemin on Rhine River not far from Holland—remained closely tied to the Abington Meeting with more than a few buried at its adjacent burial grounds. And the marriage of Wall's granddaughter, Sarah, to George Shoemaker at the Wall house in 1694 sealed the tight relationship between the families. The surrounding community that developed took on the Shoemaker family's surname.

The Shoemakertown area of Cheltenham was officially established in 1758 consisting of primarily millworkers, as various historical documents indicate. The community matured around the mill in 1746 established by Dorothy Shoemaker and Richard Mather, her brother-in-law. Later known as Charles Bosler Flour and Feed, the structure was eventually demolished.

By 1847, the home and mill "passed from the Shoemaker family to Charles Bosler, one of the [employees]. The mill was in active operation by three generations of that family, and was torn down in 1927," Lippincott noted.

Along the Tacony there were also several gristmills and a fulling mill in Cheltenham. Other sources indicate that mill communities developed in Harmer Hill near the intersection of Church Road and Limekiln Pike, as well as Milltown in what is today Cheltenham Village. And there were other milling enterprises, including C. Hammond's Tacony Edge Tool Works, which produced hammers and sledges; Rice's Mill; and finally Knight's Mill, also known as Paxsons Mill. A road that the township's Cheltenham High School rests on in the Wyncote section of the community bears the name Rice's Mill.

Charles Bosler Flour and Feed had roots to the earliest settlers in Cheltenham, particularly in the area that became known as Milltown. *Old York Road Historical Society.*

Richard Dungworth's mill was said to be one of the first, if not the original, in the area and was a primary landmark in the Milltown area of Cheltenham. *Old York Road Historical Society.*

Although the creek-side mill was demolished in 1929, the historic Shovel Shop still stands at 300 Ashbourne Road. The Pennsylvania Historical and Museum Commission in 2006 recognized the associated Thomas Rowland & Sons Shovel Works, founded by Benjamin Rowland Jr. in 1795, with a special state marker. The "millworks" operated until 1901 by the Rowland family, the plaque says. *Old York Road Historical Society.*

It's likely that Richard Dungworth built one of Cheltenham's first gristmills, perhaps the original one, in 1690 before it was later purchased by Benjamin Rowland Sr., according to township records. The mill became a booming shovel manufacturing business developed by Rowland's nephew, Benjamin Rowland Jr. By the late 1800s, T. Rowland and Sons was one of the largest producers of shovels in America. Employees who worked at the complex settled nearby, creating Milltown, which became what is today Cheltenham Village. Although the creek-side mill was demolished in 1929, the historic Shovel Shop still stands at 300 Ashbourne Road.

Meanwhile, next to Shoemakertown, another community developed called Ashbourne near Cheltenham's co-founder Toby Leech's mill that was later known as the Meyer and Ervien Fork Factory during the late 1800s.

However, European Americans weren't alone in operating gristmills and farms in Cheltenham. Remarkably, an African American established himself in the area during the late 1700s and early 1800s. "Moses Highgate was the owner and operator of a grist mill in Cheltenham Township for almost forty years," reported Reginald Pitts in his 1989 *Old York Road Historical Society Bulletin* article, "Moses Highgate, Miller of Cheltenham Township." "One of the facts that sets him apart from others of his profession is that Highgate was an Afro-American, probably one of the few that followed that craft in Pennsylvania during the nineteenth century."

REMARKABLE GENESIS OF BLACKS

A primary part of Cheltenham's early labor force, in addition to indentured servants, were black slaves and free African Americans (including Moses Highgate) used for mill and farm work, as well as other duties. Very occasionally, a local free black was able to obtain farmland and even a gristmill to operate, such as Highgate, with likely roots to enslavement.

Early Pennsylvania Quaker leaders owned slaves, including Toby Leech and the state's founder William Penn, in addition to Philadelphia's first mayor, Cheltenham resident Humphrey Morrey, whose son Richard would ignite a relationship with one of the family's slaves, Cremona, during the early 1700s at the family estate in what is today Cheltenham Township. Cremona and Richard's union would lead to the establishment of a small black town, Guineatown, which developed from the late 1700s through the 1800s, including during the Revolutionary War's Battle of Edgehill, which erupted nearby in what is today the Glenside section of Cheltenham.

Cheltenham's co-founder, Tobias Leech, clearly used slave labor to build his dynasty. His slaves, along with other "property," are even listed in his will after his death on November 13, 1727, at age seventy-four: "To his wife [Hester or Esther] he wills all his cash, silver tankard, and spoons, also forty pounds per annum during 'her pure widowhood' also his negro Cate for her own proper use, 'to dispose of as she sees fit.' The whole number of slaves he wills is eight, while the land amounts to some thousands of acres. He left several houses in Philadelphia to his sons, also his negroes, Ben, Cuffy, Betty, Cate, Cuggs, Busso and Fillis," Lippincott noted.

Leech was buried at Trinity Church on what is today Oxford Street in Philadelphia "with his wife and many descendants," after leaving to "his sons several houses in Philadelphia, more than 3,000 acres of land in Philadelphia County, and seven slaves," noted Lippincott in his book *The Mather Family of Cheltenham, Pennsylvania.* Some of those slaves were acknowledged in 2007 during Trinity ceremonies due to their long-ago burials in unmarked graves of the churchyard.

From Slavery to Guineatown

The relationship between Richard Morrey and his "housemaid" Cremona resulted in the birth of five children and the black family members' emancipation, as well as Cremona Morrey receiving in 1746 from Richard 198 acres of land—where a small black town (Guineatown) developed near what is today Arcadia University, just northwest of Philadelphia. A colonial-era family home was also built that still stands on what is today Limekiln Pike in the Glenside section of the township. An associated cemetery was established nearby, too.

Richard and Cremona eventually had their five children, despite Richard at some point being married to a woman named Ann who may have deserted him and traveled back to England with a son. Richard and Cremona's union was virtually deemed a marriage since she took on his surname of Morrey, and they likely did not hide their relationship as it developed, ultimately leading Richard to bequeath her the two hundred acres of land.

There must have been a strong element of love in the relationship, insists descendant William Pickens III, despite acknowledging that Cremona was initially enslaved by the Morrey family. Furthermore, Richard declared that Cremona and their children be liberated, one of the earliest such acts of freeing slaves in American history.

One of Cremona and Richard's five children was also named Cremona in honor of her mother. The younger Cremona married a free black man, John Montier, and one of their children, Solomon (born 1770), is a direct and modern ancestor of New York native William Pickens III (via Pickens's maternal line). Pickens has conducted far-reaching research on the family with blood links to the likes of the twentieth-century black activist Paul

Robeson, Cyrus Bustill (black baker for George Washington's Revolutionary War Continental army), David Bustill Bowser (a portrait painter of Abraham Lincoln and designer of U.S. Colored Troops Civil War regimental flags) and William Pickens Sr., a co-founder in 1909 and first field marshal of the NAACP (National Association for the Advancement of Colored People).

Interestingly enough, "Robert Lewis was the eldest child of a love affair between Richard Morrey (c. 1675–1753), the leading landowner of the area and 'his Negro Woman Mooney,' also known as Cremona," wrote Reginald Pitts in his 1991 *Old York Road Historical Society Bulletin* article "Robert Lewis of Guineatown, and 'The Colored Cemetary in Glenside.'"

Pitts further reports that Lewis was likely born between 1733 and 1735 and took the last name of a Welsh farmer in the area for whom he had worked. Lewis's brother Caesar and sisters Elizabeth, Rachael and Cremona took the surname of Murray, similar to their father Richard's surname, Morrey. Meanwhile, Robert and Caesar were apprenticed as shoemakers, possibly to neighbor Reynier Tyson. Caesar Murray later relocated to Burlington, New Jersey, working as a shoemaker and cordwainer. Robert likely worked on farms in the Guineatown area for more than a few years.

About a year after Richard's 1753 death, Cremona Sr. married an ex-slave, John Fry, with the couple having a son, Joseph. That son, Joseph, and Cremona's other children survived her. John Fry remarried a woman likely with the maiden name of Reiter, "setting off a family quarrel," according to Pitts. In fact, the Reiters, probably of German ancestry, owned land next to Cremona's original grant.

Since Cremona died intestate and left no will, a battle ensued between competing interests, including the surviving children, over the property. Essentially, Robert Lewis and his siblings (who included Cremona Morrey Jr., who had by then married the free black named John Montier) were among the beneficiaries of a 1772 agreement that required portions of the land to be divided and sold.

"John Montier arrived in Cheltenham Township in the late 1760s and married [the younger] Cremona Murray," Pitts wrote in his journal article "Robert Lewis of Guineatown." "They had four sons—Joseph (1768–1842), Solomon (1770–ca 1855), Robert (ca 1773–ca 1815 and Hiram (1780–1861). The house they lived in still stands as part of a larger home [in the 300 block of Limekiln Pike] in Glenside on the old Montier grant; tradition insists that their section was built about 1771."

Hiram Montier—a boot-maker and depicted as a finely dressed gentleman in one of two "extremely well-crafted" 1841 oil paintings recently found by

Elizabeth Brown Montier married Hiram Charles Montier in 1841, the year this oil painting was crafted by Franklin R. Street. Both portraits were discovered beneath the bed of an elderly Montier descendant and refurbished professionally several years ago by the New York–based Pickens family with roots to the Montiers. *Collection of Mr. and Mrs. William Pickens III.*

Hiram Charles Montier was a descendant of a black woman, Cremona Morrey, and Quaker landowner Richard Morrey, the son of Philadelphia's first mayor (circa 1691), Humphrey Morrey, one of the original purchasers of land in Cheltenham. Cremona had been a slave of the Morrey family before being freed and inheriting two hundred acres of land from Richard, one of the first such recorded interracial events in American history. *Collection of Mr. and Mrs. William Pickens III.*

William Pickens III and loaned to the Philadelphia Museum of Art—was Richard and Cremona's great-grandson. Hiram's wife, Elizabeth Brown Montier, is also pictured in one of the only portraits of free blacks in the North during the era of slavery and painted by a relatively unknown but extremely gifted artist, Franklin R. Street.

Over the years, Guineatown in Cheltenham continued to develop as the associated cemetery expanded with local blacks hailing from the small town, including the black Bustills, Lewises, Morreys, Montiers and Frys. Those blacks likely included "the two sons of Margaret Fry; Cuffee or Cuff Gardner, who headed a household of 'Free people other than Indians' numbering six, and Ralph Smothers, who headed a household of three," noted Pitts in the 1991 article.

Although Guineatown was physically a humble community with a cemetery, several farms, homes and the Eagle Hotel, built about 1711, it certainly nourished one of the earliest black communities in the United States. The 1790 census, according to Pitts, indicated that twenty-two people lived in Guineatown.

In fact, it's clear that members of the well-known African American Bustill family also had property interests in Guineatown. By about 1793, "We find Cyrus Bustill and Andrew Hickey being assessed for eight acres apiece while Caesar Murray is assessed three" in Guineatown, Pitts noted in the Old York Road Society's 1991 bulletin.

Cyrus Bustill was born in 1732 in Burlington, New Jersey, according to the Friends General Conference in the article "Cyrus Bustill (1732–1804)" by Vanessa Julye. He was born "enslaved" to attorney Samuel Bustill, who "sold his son to Quaker Thomas Prior, a baker who taught Cyrus his trade. Prior liberated Bustill in 1769, making him one of the 104 enslaved Africans manumitted by Friends in Burlington Quarterly Meeting of Friends from 1763–1796." Bustill would eventually bake bread for Commander George Washington to supply his Continental army during the Revolutionary War and marry "Elizabeth Morrey," likely the daughter of Richard Morrey and Cremona Morrey.

Bustill's grandson, David Bustill Bowser, would become a noted artist who painted portraits of Abraham Lincoln and the great abolitionist John Brown, as well as designed flags for the eleven black regiments of the celebrated Camp William Penn (the first and largest Federal facility to train black soldiers during the Civil War) that would later be erected in Cheltenham. And his great-great-grandson was the well-known social activist, singer, scholar and actor Paul Robeson.

Meanwhile, additional Cheltenham tax list data, according to Pitts's 1991 article, provide detailed perspectives about the dwellers of Guineatown, including Cyrus Bustill or "Bustle."

> *In 1791, classified in a separate section labeled "Mulattoes", Robert Lewis was shown to be the owner of twenty-eight acres with "dwellings", two houses and two cows. Next is John "Mountier", who contented himself with thirteen acres, his own "dwelling", one house and two cows. Following John are Andrew Hickey with thirteen acres. Cyrus "Bustle" with twelve acres, and the "Widow" Fry with four acres.*

Socialization and land transactions between Guineatown's inhabitants, or Cheltenham blacks with ties to the community, and nearby white neighbors happened from time to time, as indicative via the transfer of the two hundred acres to Cremona Morrey Sr. with the help of local Quakers serving as estate representatives.

Moses Highgate: A Trailblazing Black Miller

Without doubt, miller and farmer Moses Highgate had ties to Guineatown, a name often adopted by or given to black communities throughout parts of the United States since Africa was often referred to as "Guinea." Pitts in his Highgate article writes:

> *The land where Highgate's Mill (later Roberts' Mill) was located lay on the Cheltenham Township side of its northern boundary with Abington Township, in the area of the present* [Einstein at Elkins Park Hospital]. *The area is bounded by the present Township Line Road to the north; Jenkintown Road to the west, and Church Road to the south and east. This ground was part of the 300 acres that Everard Bolton of Ross, Herefordshire, England received from William Penn on 10 September 1683.*

Moses Highgate is also a prime example of an African American who became successful with the help of local whites since he apparently bought land and a mill from and with the assistance of neighboring Quakers in

1813. Highgate is first observed "by name in written record" in the 1798 tax list, according to Pitts's 1989 article about him, "Moses Highgate: Miller of Cheltenham Township."

It's possible that Highgate's family roots extended to a "High Gate" plantation in Gloucester County, Virginia, according to Pitts, with several relatives or siblings making their ways northward.

> *Probably of "mixed" ancestry, the Highgates could have escaped slavery or been freed through manumission, making their way to western Pennsylvania. Here they would have split forces. Moses could have headed east over the Alleghenies toward Philadelphia; Aaron heading west to Pittsburgh. Aaron Highgate eventually settled in Deer Township in Allegheny County, northwest of Pittsburgh. He soon owned a large farm, married a woman named Susanna, raised seven or eight children, and died about 1845.*

Moses Highgate could have "first settled in Tinicum Township in Delaware County (then Chester County), just south of Philadelphia," Pitts surmised, adding that he likely married "a woman named Mary Dill—at least we are sure that her first name was Mary." She may have had ties to "Thomas Dill, a Black man heading a household of four," and "listed in the 1810 Federal Census as living in [nearby] Abington Township."

Highgate fathered "at least six children, perhaps more," Pitts noted. "Since the birthdates of these children range from approximately 1785 to 1807, Highgate may have married twice during that period. It is also possible that all the following Highgates were the offspring of just one woman, Mary Dill Highgate, but no further information has yet been discerned to either support or deny this hypothesis."

However, one of Highgate's children, Susanna G. Highgate (born 1806), clearly had connections to Cheltenham's Guineatown because she married Solomon S. Montier, the ancestor of the New York–based William Pickens III whose grandfather, William Pickens Sr., co-founded in 1909 the NAACP with scholar W.E.B. Du Bois. Solomon and Susanna "lived on the family property on Limekiln Pike in what is now Glenside, until the property was sold in January 1860," just before the Civil War erupted, according to Pitts.

In order to support his wife and children, "Moses Highgate owned and operated his mill for almost thirty years and seems to have made a comfortable living for himself and family," wrote Pitts. However, upon reaching age seventy, he faced financial problems and was in great danger of losing his property.

Although a local Quaker widow, Jane Thomson, helped Highgate with finances because she had "probably known Highgate for most of her life," that was not enough. "Moses Highgate lost the mill and the three lots adjacent to it" in 1835, according to Pitts, but was able to hold on to his house and "three-quarters of an acre of land, with a horse, a cow, and a dog."

Then on October 1, 1837, "Mrs. Thomson sold the mill to [Jehu Jones Roberts] for $2,600. He worked the mill for about thirty years, eventually selling out to the Roland family," Pitts reported.

Moses Highgate and his family resided in the house near Church Road for a few more years. However, on December 18, 1841, Moses and wife Mary sold the home to their son William for just ten dollars, likely as collateral for a grocery store the son operated and owned, Pitts surmised. However, less than a year later on July 25, 1842, Moses Highgate died at age seventy-eight from a short but severe illness.

Yet as Pitts points out, the story of Moses Highgate is so compelling because he was likely "the only [African American] millowner in Cheltenham Township during the heyday of the mills that once provided its major industry." The "courage and desire of Moses Highgate to attempt establishing and continuing a thriving business, and of the help of those Friends…who gave both financial and moral support to aid in his success" is a fine example of early racial unity in Cheltenham and, for that matter, in America.

Meanwhile, racial relations overall in America—despite local Quakers mostly opposing slavery by the time of Highgate's death—still had a way to go. By 1850 the second infamous Fugitive Slave Act empowered so-called slave catchers to re-enslave or capture runaway blacks in virtually any U.S. locale, undoubtedly affecting the lives of blacks in Guineatown and Philadelphia, with the largest urban African American population in the United States.

The ensuing fury of black and white abolitionists sent the country into an uproar as many slaves escaped plantations via the Underground Railroad, a secret system that harbored runaways, including the likes of Frederick Douglass and Harriet Tubman, the soon-to-be matriarch of the system. An epicenter of that system would be located in Cheltenham Township through the local homestead of the white Quaker Lucretia Mott and her family. It was on the land of her son-in-law, Edward M. Davis, where the first and largest erected facility to train black soldiers during the Civil War, Camp William Penn, would be built in 1863. And it was a place where Douglass, Tubman and even William Still, "the father of the Underground Railroad," would be forever linked.

However, almost a century before the Civil War, the issues of America's independence had to be addressed first. As American colonists during the 1770s and 1780s pulled away from England and created the Declaration of Independence and subsequent U.S. Constitution, the likes of George Washington and Thomas Jefferson, both slaveholders like Cheltenham's Toby Leech, realized that America's failure to liberate blacks would eventually come back to haunt the nation. Such Americans believed that their personal and the country's immediate fortunes depended on slavery, more than likely a very hot topic in such communities as Cheltenham's Guineatown.

Consequently, local Philadelphia blacks, including Cyrus Bustill (with property in Guineatown and Philadelphia) and James Forten, who would actually fight in the Revolutionary War before becoming a wealthy sail maker, eventually pressed forward with the early black freedom movement and their trailblazing organization, the Free African Society, co-founded by black preachers Absalom Jones and Richard Allen.

Battling for Liberty: The Age of George Washington and Battle of Edge Hill

There's little doubt that the black inhabitants of Guineatown and other Cheltenham citizens heard the gunshots of British and American forces as they clashed over the Edge Hill highlands in the vicinity of the Montier home and Guineatown on December 7, 1777. In fact, elements of both armies reportedly drank from a spring at the intersection of what is today Church Road and Washington Lane during the combat, according to historical documents and a commemorative plaque located at the intersection.

As British forces moved toward Philadelphia and positioned themselves to overtake Washington's forces, Hessian soldiers fighting with the English king's forces "committed great outrages on the inhabitants, particularly at John Shoemaker's…a well-to-do farmer and miller, whose home and grist mill was beside the York Road" that dated to 1746, wrote Henry Melchior Muhlenberg in his 1908 book *The Pennsylvania-German in the Revolutionary War*.

The British were outraged as Howe's troops frustratingly looked for an opening in the American lines, soon lighting torches and burning local residences, clearly riling residents in Philadelphia's Germantown and even in the Cheltenham vicinity.

The American and British forces fought and maneuvered to take the highlands of the Edge Hill area with both sides suffering about forty casualties, according to historical sources. Two American commanders, General John Cadwalader and Colonel Joseph Reed, were rescued by a squadron of American troops led by Captain Allen McLane, when they were pinned down in a wooded area and about to be captured or killed. Although the Continental army's Morgan's Rangers, known as very adept sharpshooters, conducted guerilla-type maneuvers, the British were able to hold their own before both sides withdrew.

About the time Washington wrote Congress concerning the Battle of Edge Hill during the frigid winter of 1777, his army was camped at Whitemarsh, where the British were planning to attack.

According to several sources, a local Quaker woman, Lydia Darragh, reportedly heard the plans for the attack and walked over snow-covered roads and gave her information to Lieutenant Colonel Craig and General Elias Boudinot at Rising Sun Inn. Washington was warned by soldiers who likely traveled up York Road and then west on Church Road in order to reach Washington's Whitemarsh headquarters quickly.

American forces, by December 19, were forced to leave and camp in Valley Forge for a brutal winter without sufficient rations, which would lead to virtual starvation and the brink of defeat. Yet the mighty efforts of citizens like the black baker Cyrus Bustill and Quaker Lydia Darragh would help the Americans to live to fight another day.

They are indicative of the many Cheltenham warriors who fought for this country in virtually every war, extending from the American Revolution through the world wars and beyond. Indeed, war memorials on Tookany Drive near Cheltenham Village, in the Curtis Arboretum and in the heart of LaMott recognize veterans who gave blood for liberty.

From Ancient Pathways to Stagecoach Roads

Many of the very roads that Washington's army traversed—originally paths of Native Americans and subsequently used by early European hunters, farmers and mill operators—were developed into modern thoroughfares.

For instance, York Road (circa 1711) was the first such passageway in Cheltenham Township that "abounded in quicksand and mud holes, and in the spring of the year, and during the winter, farmers who used the road to take their produce to market would have to wait until as many as six teams could be hitched together to negotiate the mudholes," according to Morgan's 1945 essay "Preserving the Heritage of Cheltenham Township," based on his November 21, 1944 presentation to the Old York Road Historical Society and published in the group's bulletin.

Such developing roads had "overseers," including Bartholomew Mather starting in 1707, as well as Alexander Loller and Thomas Shoemaker in 1785, according to *Bean's History of Montgomery County*. As time moved on, the Old York Road later became a "turnpike." The Cheltenham and Willow Grove Turnpike, as it was called, stretched eleven miles in length on the York Road and cost thousands of dollars to build.

Numerous businesses developed along what became known as Old York Road, a toll road until 1928. In fact, there were actually toll gates at City

Posing for his 100th birthday, Isaac Mather sits near his son Israel, the great-great-grandson of Joseph Mather, according to the Old York Road Historical Society. Isaac lived virtually through the entire nineteenth century, born on October 27, 1806, and dying on November 23, 1907. *Old York Road Historical Society.*

Line [today Cheltenham Avenue] and what is today Ogontz Avenue. Old York Road, early on, was also a stagecoach route extending to metropolitan New York.

Mapmaker John Hill would survey Cheltenham and the Philadelphia area, creating the *Map of Philadelphia and Environs* from 1801 through 1807, published in 1809. It was probably the first local map of its kind, incorporating Lower Merion and 60 percent of Cheltenham.

G.H. Hopkins would publish atlases of Montgomery County that included an 1871 version with "103 pages of colored maps" that was "the first atlas on the county," according to Bean. Another 1877 atlas of 89 pages included "the consolidated city," and "farm maps" of area townships, including Cheltenham, as well as nearby "Abington…Springfield, Whitemarsh, Plymouth, Norriton, Lower Merion and the borough of Norristown; also parts of Moreland, Upper Dublin, Whitpain, Montgomery, Worcester and Upper Merion."

Meanwhile, Easton Road was developed from "Willow Grove to Warrington in 1722, and later to Doylestown," Morgan noted. That road also "extended to Germantown, thus being one of Cheltenham's early roads," encompassing the business district of Glenside, originally Edge Hill.

Then there's the essential Limekiln Pike that was constructed in 1716. The name came about because the road led to the lime kilns near Fitzwatertown. The lime was essential for constructing many buildings in the area, quite possibly including the statehouse or Independence Hall.

Actually, the history of Church Road is inseparable from Cheltenham's rich past. Laid out in 1734, it connects the Bethlehem Pike and the Skippack Pike, constructed in 1714 to connect with Philadelphia's Frankford community. As the story goes, Morgan told Old York Road Historical Society members in 1944: "The St. Thomas Church in Whitemarsh had been founded, but could not afford to pay a minister. Trinity Church in Oxford had been organized, and likewise could not afford to pay a minister. The two churches therefore joined in bringing over from England a clergyman [George Keith] who preached one Sunday at one church and the alternate Sunday at the other, and naturally the road between the two was the result." And as noted earlier, Cheltenham's co-founder, Toby Leech, and his family became members of Trinity.

Another major Cheltenham thoroughfare, Washington Lane, according to Morgan, "was laid out in 1734, being the most convenient and direct route for the Quakers to travel between Abington and Germantown." During the Battle of Germantown with the British, according to Morgan, a column of Washington's army marched "on Germantown on the existing roads, the Ridge Pike, the Germantown Pike, Church Road, the York Road and Limekiln Pike. So again, the roads of Cheltenham echoed to the marching feet of the American patriot army."

Finally, Cheltenham Avenue, originally known as Township Line Road, was likely very early a Native American path that ultimately became the official dividing line between Philadelphia and the township, incorporated in 1900. The historic black community of LaMott, named after the famed white Quaker antislavery abolitionist Lucretia Mott, is situated along a north-side sector of west Cheltenham Avenue. Her home Roadside was located along Old York Road, a few blocks north of Cheltenham Avenue with land abutting what is today Cheltenham Avenue.

EARLY WEALTH DEVELOPMENT

Commerce growth in the township can be traced back to the days of Leech and Wall, as well as the period of the American Revolution. The 1776 tax assessment of Cheltenham and various business profiles examined in *Bean's History of Montgomery County* and elsewhere are very revealing.

The Revolutionary War–era evaluation of property owners—many of them associated with the area's mills and farms—indicates that Peter Rush was the collector and Bartholomew Mather, the assessor, with the latter having ties to the historic Mather family of Cheltenham.

There are several Shoemakers who developed the booming mill community along the Tookany waterway listed in the assessment, including George Shoemaker with ninety-three acres, four horses and five cows. William Shoemaker had fifty-five acres, two horses and two cows.

The assessor himself, Bartholomew Mather, was listed with 93 acres, three horses, four cows, as well as "1/2 saw-mill" and "1/2 gristmill." Richard Mather, a likely relative, had 120 acres, a servant, four horses and eight cows, as well as half a sawmill and gristmill, making it probable that he co-owned those properties with Bartholomew.

Among the largest property owners, according to the list, appear to be descendants of Toby Leech and his children, including Samuel Leech with 170 acres, three horses and five cows; Jacob Leech with 168 acres, two servants, three horses and four cows; and Jacob Miller with 200 acres, three servants, four horses and five cows.

In addition to Toby Leech owning slaves very early in Cheltenham's history, as examined previously, there were several others in the Cheltenham area still involved in human bondage in 1776—decades after Quakers began to eradicate slavery in the area—including Joseph Linn, with eighty-four acres, "1 negro," a horse and four cows and Richard Martin, a tanner, with forty-six acres, a tanyard, "1 servant, 1 Negro," three horses and three cows.

Other interesting sketches of early wealth and property holders in Cheltenham, according to Bean and other sources, include the following.

Albert J. Engle was a very respected entrepreneur of Cheltenham's Shoemakertown. Born on January 2, 1826, he learned to become a stonemason before marrying Annetta Megargee of Cheltenham in 1849. By 1850, the couple operated a thriving mercantile business in a store that was operated by Richard Shoemaker. In the need for more space, the couple soon purchased a property once owned by the Tyson family, building a large and well-stocked store. Engle was later appointed postmaster of Shoemakertown.

Samuel M. Wilson was born on January 12, 1840, working mostly as a laborer on farms and acquiring a limited education. After renting a farm in Bucks County in 1866, he started a grocery business in Philadelphia. It wasn't long before he relocated to Edge Hill and opened a country store. He also became the local postmaster before investing in mining iron ore.

Thomas T. Mather, part of a very historic family in the area, was born in Cheltenham on February 7, 1814, to Jonathan Mather and Elizabeth Tyson Mather of Edge Hill. The family farmed, although he was provided a very good education. In fact, Mather had a "mathematical mind" and was very proficient in science. However, he preferred to be a farmer, a profession in which he excelled. Realizing his business acumen, Mather became a director of the Jenkintown National Bank and Germantown National Bank and had leadership responsibilities with the Limekiln Turnpike Company. He was also treasurer of the Chelton Hills Mutual Improvement Association. He died on June 21, 1877, as a devout Quaker and member of the Abington Monthly Meeting.

C. Hammond established in Shoemakertown in 1842 the reputable C. Hamond & Sons Machinists. The firm for many years manufactured "hammers, edge-tools, railroad, machinists and blacksmiths' tools." With offices on North Fifth Street in Philadelphia, the primary "works" was

Built about 1893, the C.M. Case store sold vegetables, meats and other groceries, as well as various "provisions." It was possibly designed by Horace Trumbauer, according to the Old

York Road Historical Society. Several patrons, proprietors and children pose in this early 1900s image—along with a couple of working horses. *Old York Road Historical Society.*

Founded in 1924 by Francis Richard Taylor, the Cheltenham National Bank's five-dollar note was issued during the Roaring Twenties. Taylor also co-founded the reconstituted Cheltenham Friends Meeting about 1915. *Old York Road Historical Society.*

"situated in Cheltenham township, on Tacony Creek," according to Bean. "The firm commenced with fifteen hands and a pay-roll of five hundred dollars a month. They now [in 1884] employ seventy hands, with [its] pay-roll of two thousand five hundred dollars a month…The motive-power is supplied by a seventy horse-power steam-engine and a water-wheel of twenty horse-power." The property sat on 1.5 acres.

William Moore established the Cheltenham Coach-Works, also in Shoemakertown, near the York Road Station in 1870. The four-story property had thirty-five "hands" and "a pay-roll of fifteen hundred dollars per month," according to Bean. "The work made consists of phaetons, wagons, carriages, buggies, etc.; the whole process, from the rough wood-work to the most artistic painting and upholstering, is performed on the premises."

Myers & Ervien of Shoemakertown, a major fork maker along with other items, was started in 1848 by Jacob Myers, whose father Jacob Sr., with roots to Germany, served in the Revolutionary War "under General Washington." The younger Myers started the firm with just a half-dozen

A Cheltenham gentleman, Robert E. Blake, enjoys a carriage ride, taking a moment in history near the turn of the last century to pose for a snapshot. *Old York Road Historical Society.*

workers. By 1850, John A. Ervien became a partner, giving the firm a great boost. Meyers, in fact, became a soldier in the Civil War, fighting in major battles in the Army of the Potomac. The firm's "works" were located along Tacony Creek. The two-acre property included several important plants. In 1884, there were fifty-five employees for the firm with a monthly payroll of $2,500.

Central to Cheltenham's early business development was the Cheltenham Roller Mills, also located in Shoemakertown and the "property of Charles Bosler & Son," with a "history dating back to old Revolutionary times." Indeed the location, according to Bean, was "in the centre of one of the best agricultural sections of the State and of the county." The mill had the capacity to produce 150 barrels of flour in a twenty-four-hour period. The mill was originally "built jointly by Dorothy Shoemaker, Richard Mathers and John Tyson, on the property of Dorothy Shoemaker, in whose family the grounds had been held from the time of William Penn." The deed dated back to 1746, according to Bean.

Charles B. Wright was one of the most prominent businesspersons of Cheltenham, rising to become a major developer of U.S. railroads and president of the Northern Pacific. He maintained and lived in huge Philadelphia and Cheltenham estates, splitting his residency equally in both mansions. He was of Quaker ancestry and born in Bradford County, Pennsylvania, on January 8, 1822. "He embarked in business while a mere boy, and at the age of twenty years he was a successful merchant and banker in Western Pennsylvania," said his obituary in the March 25, 1898 edition of the *New York Times*. As the primary director and then president of the Northern Pacific Railroad "he did effective work in pushing the road to completion," and following the "failure of the firm of Jay Cooke & Co.," he "assisted in thc reorganization, by which the [railroad] was completed to Puget Sound." He's even credited with founding the city of Tacoma, whcre he endowed educational institutions. Wright died in March 1898.

Wright was among an elite class of super-entrepreneurs who settled in Cheltenham, including Jay Cooke, the aforementioned "financier of the Civil War" for the Union, and Edward M. Davis, the son-in-law of Lucretia Mott—setting the stage for the splendiferous Gilded Age in Cheltenham. It was a community destined to become one of the wealthiest in the nation, as local roads, railways and neighborhoods developed, featuring stellar mansions built with almost inestimable wealth and designed by the country's greatest architects. Some observers dubbed the area as having the most millionaires per square mile than any other community in the United States. Among those Cheltenham elite were John B. Stetson, the hat maker; ice cream producer Henry Breyer; and department store magnate John Wannamaker, as well as transportation industrialist partners William McIntire Elkins and P.A.B. Widener.

PART II

AN EPIC CIVIL WAR AND DEMANDING LIBERTY

To understand the development of the Gilded Age's high society in Cheltenham, it's imperative to focus on influential Quakers in the area, their social initiatives and the township's involvement in the Civil War, most notably the establishment in summer 1863 of the first and largest Federal facility to train black soldiers during that "war of the Rebellion." Those developments correlate with the involvement of the Quaker and Cheltenham land developer Edward M. Davis, as well as the position of his famous mother-in-law, the renowned Quaker minister, Lucretia Mott, who was a pioneering antislavery abolitionist and women's rights advocate during the mid- to late 1800s and who settled on Old York Road.

As Quakers throughout the region moved away from slavery during the mid-1700s, led by the likes of early trailblazers John Woolman, Benjamin Lay and Daniel Pastorius, such antislavery activities were vigorously picked up by Lucretia Mott and her son-in-law Edward, as well as other family members and associates through the 1800s. Pastorius, who converted to Quakerism, wrote in 1688 the first recorded protest against slavery in America with some backing from the Cheltenham, Abington and other meetinghouses in Philadelphia.

For sure, the Cheltenham and Abington areas attracted more than a few Quakers with antislavery sentiments, including Lay, who lived in a cave along what is today Old York Road in Abington during the mid-1700s and protested or stirred the consciousness of Quaker slaveholders at meeting places and even on the Philadelphia streets. His freedom-fighting trail often traversed Cheltenham. So the Cheltenham area, in many ways, was quite an appropriate area for Lucretia Mott.

LUCRETIA MOTT: THE ULTIMATE FREEDOM FIGHTER

Known during her heyday as the most recognized female abolitionist and women's rights advocate in America, Lucretia Coffin Mott was born on January 3, 1793, on Nantucket Island, Massachusetts, to Quakers Thomas Coffin and Anna Folger (a distant cousin to the colonial luminary Benjamin Franklin, who had become an antislavery abolitionist likely influenced by Benjamin Lay despite his earlier slavery involvement). Since Lucretia's father Thomas operated the whaling ship *Trial*, his absence during long voyages allowed his wife and daughters to develop a great sense of independence, similar to women of other whaling families on the island.

Lucretia's parents apparently groomed her independent streak, although her mother sometimes dubbed Lucretia as "Long-Tongue" and her biographer, Margaret Bacon, a descendant, described the young lady as "a very human person with a quick temper, a sharp tongue, and a stubborn streak."

Standing under five feet as an adult, after receiving a very good education and grades at Quaker schools or academies Lucretia became an assistant teacher at the New York–based Nine Partners Boarding School, where she finished her studies in 1808 at about age fifteen.

Soon she'd meet a teacher there, James Mott Jr., about age twenty, who was reserved and quite tall. Yet the outspoken and spirited Lucretia found him attractive, and they married on April 10, 1811, and lived briefly in New York City before traveling to Philadelphia, where her mother, Anna, had opened a store and boardinghouse following her husband's death.

Mott's husband, James, opened a successful wholesale business in Philadelphia that specialized in domestic and foreign goods, allowing the couple to move out of Anna Mott's home and purchase their own abode on Samson Street. It was a meeting place for well-known abolitionists, including the great William Lloyd Garrison, who convinced the Motts to actively fight for the emancipation of slaves. Garrison, at that time, was America's best-known antislavery activist.

Mott was a voracious reader, influenced by activists Sarah Zane, a popular Philadelphia Quaker, and Elias Hicks, who would formulate the Hicksite sect of Quakers fiercely dedicated to combating slavery. Mott became a fierce ally of Hicks, whose branch separated from the main body of the Friends during the schism of 1827. She was also greatly influenced by the thoughts of Mary Wollstonecraft and her book *A Vindication of the Rights of Women*. By the early 1830s, Lucretia Coffin Mott had become a sought-after traveling Quaker minister who reportedly did not bother her husband, James, sharing her view that marriages should be egalitarian.

Mott co-founded the Philadelphia Female Anti-Slavery Society in 1833 and in 1835 the National Anti-Slavery Coalition of American Women. Although Mott was unhappy about women not being able to join male antislavery abolitionist groups at that point, both female groups enjoyed the memberships of black women, including Hattie Purvis, Sarah Douglas and several from the Forten family.

Despite horrific proslavery mob violence in Boston, New York and Philadelphia, an abolitionist headquarters (Pennsylvania Hall) was built 1838 in Philadelphia but soon set aflame by racists. They were particularly angry about the mixed-race and mixed-gender meetings—gatherings that some historians believed spawned the women's rights movement. Even the great poet John Greenleaf Whittier, who visited the Motts in 1838 and opened an antislavery newspaper office in Philadelphia, was shut down after his place was set afire. Meanwhile, the Mottses' home was also threatened.

Still, the Motts also associated with known conductors of the Underground Railroad, including William Still, who wrote the epic book *The Underground Railroad*. The manuscript was based on helping and interviewing hundreds of escaped slaves along the secretive routes of woodland and riverbank paths, as well as in hay-covered wagons to secret locations, including the Mottses' Philadelphia-area residences. There's even evidence that Edward M. Davis and other abolitionists, quite likely including Lucretia and James Mott, helped with the September 1838 escape of a Maryland slave, Frederick Douglass, destined to become the major black spokesperson of his time. Douglass would briefly stay in Philadelphia during that escape on his way to New York City. And it's no coincidence that the matriarch or "Moses" of the Underground Railroad, Harriet Tubman, ended up in Philadelphia and soon associated with the Motts after her escape in 1849, just one year before the infamous Fugitive Slave Act. All of those antislavery abolitionists and Underground Railroad constituents, in fact, would one day be linked to Camp William Penn.

However, by 1844, suffering from chronic influenza and encephalitis that caused her weight to drop to ninety-two pounds, Lucretia Mott received an impressive stream of well-wishers at her home in the 100 block of Ninth Street in Philadelphia, including Charles Dickens, Ralph Waldo Emerson, Benjamin Lundy, John Quincy Adams, William Lloyd Garrison, Sojourner Truth, Robert and Hattie Purvis, Miller McKim and many more.

By 1850, when the Fugitive Slave Act went into effect that allowed slave-catchers to virtually send any black person back to slavery (and in many cases for the first time), Mott was in great demand as a public speaker. She also became involved with several epic antislavery and pro–women rights' meetings and organizations, including the American Anti-Slavery Society in New York and the Seneca Falls meeting for women's rights with the likes of Elizabeth Cady Stanton.

The Great Mott Abolitionists Make Cheltenham Home

Lucretia Mott's fragile health and son-in-law Edward M. Davis's property holdings in Chelten Hills (eventually known as part of Cheltenham Township), just northwest of Philadelphia, would prompt the family in 1854 to move to the home Roadside along Old York Road, just north of Township Line Road (today Cheltenham Avenue).

As the country fractured more over the Fugitive Slave Act and the debate about slavery spread west, John Brown, the white abolitionist, led a group of whites and blacks on the Harpers Ferry raid in 1859 but was arrested, destined for the gallows. His wife, Mary, stayed with the Motts during part of that very difficult time and even received correspondence from her doomed husband at the Mottses' residence: "I remember the old lady well; but presume has no recollection of me…I am glad to have you make the acquaintance of such old Pioneers in the Cause," John Brown wrote to his wife.

Although Mott abhorred bloodshed and did not actively support it during the Civil War, she was well aware that the Federal government would lease property that son-in-law Edward M. Davis owned to erect Camp William Penn. Initially

Lucretia Mott's Roadside home was a major station on the Underground Railroad. *Old York Road Historical Society.*

built on land owned by the financier Jay Cooke, the site was moved to Davis's more level land. It would be the first and largest Federal facility erected during the war to train black soldiers. In fact, Davis served as a captain at the start of the war under General John Fremont, in Missouri territory, when his commander issued an order in 1861 that slaves be liberated in the region, something that President Abraham Lincoln thought to be too premature for fear of enraging Southern states and proslavery elements in western territories. Lincoln, according to several historical sources, dismissed Fremont (a future candidate for U.S. president) from his post, angering the likes of the Mottses and Captain Davis.

Locally, and in Pennsylvania, authorities at the start of the war in 1861 refused to allow blacks to form regiments. Many Pennsylvania and Philadelphia-area blacks traveled to Massachusetts and joined the African American state militias being formed, the Fifty-fifth and Fifty-fourth Massachusetts (of motion picture *Glory* fame). And although the Fifty-fourth was memorialized as fierce combatants and recognized in its losing battle at South Carolina's Fort Wagner, other Union losses began to imperil the Union as Lincoln early on held off using Federal black troops to help the cause.

Lincoln by 1863 realized that the Union was in desperate trouble as Confederate forces swept into Pennsylvania and threatened Philadelphia, as well as Washington, D.C., leading to the monumental Battle of Gettysburg.

Union organizations, in support of Lincoln, began to form throughout the United States, including in Philadelphia. The Union League of Philadelphia, in fact, included the likes of Edward M. Davis, who with other antislavery advocates in the organization helped to raise funds to allow black soldiers to support the beleaguered Union army. That was as Frederick Douglass convinced the president that black men, on the Federal level, were ready to fight heartily for their independence and to save the Union. Further, Douglass and other black leaders rationalized that it was a grand opportunity for blacks to earn equality and citizenship.

RAGING CIVIL WAR AND THE FOUNDING OF CAMP WILLIAM PENN

Finally, during the summer of 1863, Abraham Lincoln's Bureau of United States Colored Troops was formed, and an officers' candidate school for white officers to train the black soldiers was instituted in downtown Philadelphia at 1210 Chestnut Street. By then, thousands of free blacks and ex-slaves were rushing to enlist in the Union army, many of them pouring through the gates of Camp William Penn.

The enthusiasm was electric, according to a witness, First Lieutenant Oliver Norton of the camp's Eighth United States Colored Troops (USCT)

This early image of Camp William Penn's grounds (circa 1863–64) reveals the expansiveness of the site and structures that may have been later used to construct La Mott residences. *Historical Society of Pennsylvania.*

Renowned as the most well-known African American of his time, Frederick Douglass spoke at Camp William Penn and was a close friend to the white Quaker antislavery abolitionist who lived nearby, Lucretia Mott. *Library of Congress.*

Regiment: "There are hundreds of them, mostly slaves, here by now, anxiously waiting for the recruiting officer. The boys are singing: 'Rally round the flag, boys, rally once again, shouting the battle cry of freedom, down with the traitor, up with the star.'"

However, such antislavery fervor did not mean pro-Confederate elements weren't apparent in Philadelphia or, for that matter, in southeastern Pennsylvania. As early as 1842, Frederick Douglass, shortly after escaping slavery, was pulled from a Norristown train by a racist passenger after giving a speech, and at one point he was nearly beaten to death, with Lucretia Mott and other abolitionists nursing him back to health. In fact, area streetcars and trains were segregated, with several black leaders and white abolitionists (including Lucretia Mott) protesting the practice.

Standing beside Mott was Camp William Penn's commander, Louis Wagner, a young officer of German ancestry who despised slavery; he was earlier injured and captured in the Second Battle of Bull Run on August 30, 1862. After returning to Union forces via a prisoner exchange, by early 1863 he volunteered to take command of Camp William Penn, which was

Louis Wagner, the commander of Camp William Penn, advocated for his black soldiers and fought against segregation. Following the Civil War, he became an important civic, political and educational leader in Philadelphia. *U.S. Army Military History Institute.*

to be situated on eleven acres of Edward M. Davis's land in the rolling hills of Chelten Hills.

Indeed, Wagner was likely on hand when Douglass, a paid Union recruiter, entered the grounds in July 1863 as other Philadelphians in South Carolina fought with the Massachusetts Fifty-fourth, as well as Douglass's sons, who had joined that regiment. The Fifty-fourth would sustain horrible losses, with its commander, Robert Gould Shaw, dying. Many of his black soldiers were buried together with him in a mass grave.

As Douglass prepared to speak to the first black brigade to be trained at Camp William Penn, the Third USCT, he noticed several black recruits standing on top of barrels with rails over their shoulders as punishment for various military misdeeds.

Douglass was clearly upset when he addressed the Third Regiment troops because he had learned that some of the men—many bearing the scars of slavery—were giving white officers difficulty. One disgusted officer condemned the ability of the black recruits to become decent soldiers.

Then Douglass began to speak, with his voice rumbling over the Chelten Hills landscape: "The fortunes of the whole race for generations to come are bound up in the success or failure of the 3rd Regiment of colored troops from the North," he said. "You are a spectacle for men and angels. You are in a manner to answer the question, can the black man be a soldier?"

His answer was precise and forceful: "That we can now make soldiers of these men, there can be no doubt!"

Douglass was obviously concerned about Copperheads and local proslavery antagonists waiting to exploit any perceived negative development at Camp William Penn. Hence he was troubled about the rebellious attitudes of some of the new black soldiers—even if they were justified by reacting to the racism of white officers or medical personnel. Douglass urged the men to look at the big picture and make immediate sacrifices to achieve overall liberty for black Americans.

The first regiment to train at Camp William Penn, the Third USCT, would soon leave for war on September 18, 1863, as autumn settled in the Chelten Hills highlands. The departure was not before the regiment faced other racist obstacles in early August, such as not being permitted to parade as white troops had done while marching off to war. Local officials were afraid of inciting whites in fear of so many blacks with weapons and strutting in uniforms, as reported in the August 7, 1863 edition of the *Christian Recorder*, an African American newspaper published by the African American Methodist Episcopal Church.

In the intervening time, back at the training grounds in Cheltenham, the soldiers complained of being mistreated, with several even writing to President Abraham Lincoln about malicious medical officers at Camp William Penn and voting disenfranchisement.

Yet even Lucretia Mott, who did not officially support violence and war due to her Quaker pacifist beliefs, noted the progress of the soldiers at the facility, where she was known to speak and even give fresh pies and other goodies to the troops. She accepted an invitation to preach at Camp William Penn in the summer of 1863, noted a Mott descendant, Margaret Hope Bacon, in the 1980 book *Valiant Friend: The Life of Lucretia Mott.*

> *Whatever she thought of war, she believed these young black soldiers, too, needed her spiritual comfort. On July 12 she walked over to the camp from Roadside and was shown by the commanding officer where she could stand on some boxes (local legend has it that it was a drum) so that, small as she was, she could be seen and heard. Then some six hundred soldiers were marched in formation before her. She spoke to them stressing the theme of the one true religion and her own faith that the time would come when war would be no more.*

Meanwhile, the camp's commander, Louis Wagner, sometimes conferred with Mott and generally shared her antislavery sentiments while fiercely supporting his men, even in the face of strong public pressure. He supported the efforts to desegregate local horse-drawn trolleys and trains, as well as other public accommodations.

When a black sentry (Private Charles Ridley) of the camp shot a quarrelsome white man, William Fox, who lived in the neighborhood, Wagner came to the soldier's defense—though a trial was eventually held in the county seat of Norristown, resulting in a minimal sentence for the soldier despite wide publicity.

Locally, members of St. Paul's Episcopal Church, which Jay Cooke had co-founded, helped out with supplies and spiritual needs, directed by its first rector, Reverend J. Parvin.

On top of that, Commander Wagner's brother, George, who also served in a Camp William Penn regiment, the Eighth USCT, had strong abolitionist tendencies and a tough battle record. He would get wounded during the Eighth Regiment's February 1864 Battle of Olustee in Florida, when the brigade suffered terrible losses, including 343 killed, wounded or missing in action.

Despite the Eighth and several other USCT regiments being inadequately trained, many did meet the test of battle, including the Sixth USCT of Camp William Penn, which even paraded down Philadelphia's central road, Broad Street, and by the Union League's front steps filled with hotshot military brass and civilian officials.

One observer said, despite a young tough unsuccessfully trying to snatch the colors: "Walnut, Pine and Broad Streets listened to the measured tread of the dusky soldiers and the staccato of a full drum corps. The Union blue, the white gloves and the glint of fixed bayonets contrasted sharply with the dark faces perspiring under the rays of a warm October sun."

The regiment would soon face much tougher tests with its regimental flag during battle; it was designed by the highly esteemed black artist David Bustill Bowser, who had roots to the family of Cyrus Bustill and who had baked for George Washington's army less than one century earlier. Time and time again the enemy would try to take the regiment's colors depicting the Goddess of Liberty holding a flag while exhorting a black freeman dressed as a soldier to fight with vigor and determination.

On the nippy and misty September 29, 1864 morning, the Sixth Regiment was destined to make history during the Battle of New Market Heights or Chaffin's farm in Virginia. More than 60 percent of the regiment's men would

Engraved by P.S. Duval and Son in Philadelphia, the design of this recruiting poster for black troops was based on an earlier photograph of Camp William Penn soldiers of the Twenty-fifth United States Colored Troops. *Library Company of Philadelphia.*

die in battle, with several earning the prestigious Medal of Honor, including officer Nathan H. Edgerton, Sergeant Alexander Kelly and Sergeant Major Thomas Hawkins, all credited with saving the regimental colors.

There were other regiments of Camp William Penn with notable accomplishments, including the Twenty-second that served in Virginia and was one of the initial regiments to march into the Confederate capital of Richmond. That group also led the funeral of the beloved president, Abraham Lincoln, after his April 1865 assassination following the war.

The members of the Twenty-fourth Regiment in February 1865 would even listen to an inspiring speech by the tremendous Underground Railroad matriarch Harriet Tubman as the war wound down, just before they would take to the field. Her presence at the camp, along with such abolitionists as William Still, Robert Purvis, William Lloyd Garrison, John Greenleaf Whittier and many others, is a clear indication that the so-called Camptown section of Cheltenham was an epicenter of the Underground Railroad. Reports of tunnels beneath the earth near the past site of Mott's Roadside estate suggest the escape routes of enslaved

Africans who often moved toward Lancaster County and then New York before heading to Canada, the "Promised Land." Indeed, it's not beyond imagination that Tubman would have led to freedom some of the very men before her.

Other regiments of the eleven that organized in Cheltenham—including the 32nd, 41st, 43rd, 45th and 127th—fought in Virginia's Battle of the Crater, saw combat at Petersburg and Richmond and engaged in the Battles of Darbytown Road, Deep Bottom and Fair Oaks, as well as Hatcher's Run. They also served in South Carolina, including at Hilton Head, Port Royal, Otter Island, Fenwick Island, North Edisto Island and James Island. Some would corner Lee's army and watch the general's surrender at Appomattox, a very rewarding experience since many were former slaves. Still others would march with the Union general, William Tecumseh Sherman, who is credited with leaving much of the South in flames. Many of the Camp William Penn soldiers would serve their final days in Texas near the Mexican border. A few would join the elite Buffalo soldiers and rack up further combat experience on the western frontier against the Native Americans.

Lucretia Mott's Pinnacle and Exceptional Legacy

As the war wound down, Jay Cooke, who lived not far from Camp William Penn in a grand mansion that he named Ogontz, would receive visits from the winning Union general Ulysses Grant. His son Jesse attended a local school, the Cheltenham Military Academy, which is today the headquarters of the school district on the southeast corner of Washington Lane and Ashbourne Road. The great Lucretia Mott would also visit Cooke, with the trio once discussing the plight of Native Americans.

Greatly concerned about the Native Americans being placed on reservations and annihilated by westward-moving expansionists, Mott urged President Grant not to allow the execution of six so-called rebellious Indians of the California-based Modoc tribe. She managed to save the lives of two.

Mott, in fact, became extraordinarily involved in the women's rights movement, often entertaining at her residence the likes of Susan B. Anthony, Lucy Stone and Elizabeth Cady Stanton, just to name a few superstars of the movement who touched down in Cheltenham.

The village of La Mott in Cheltenham was named for Lucretia Mott, the most recognized woman during her era, dedicated to rights of women and African Americans. *Library of Congress.*

Sometimes called the "Black Man's Goddess," Mott had ties to the women's rights movement early on when in the summer of 1853 she introduced as speakers at the Women's Rights Convention the "round-faced Lucy Stone and sharp-featured Susan B. Anthony, co-workers with Lucretia in the woman's rights movement," noted Bacon. And despite numerous interruptions by "rowdies" making "catcalls and jibes," Mott kept relative order, exclaiming, "Any great change must expect opposition, because it shakes the very foundation of privilege."

As the meeting continued, Mott eventually introduced the great abolitionist Sojourner Truth, "a tall black woman, an ex-slave, who had electrified a woman's rights convention in Akron, Ohio, the year before" with the speech, "Ain't I a Woman?" In fact, Truth, who would visit Roadside in Cheltenham, directly addressed the increasingly hostile crowd: "I know it feels kind of hissin' and ticklin' like to see a colored woman get up and tell you about things, and woman's rights. We have all been thrown down so low that nobody thought we'd ever get up again, but we have been down long enough now; we will come up again, and here I am."

However, by the time the meeting adjourned, the activists, including William Lloyd Garrison, black minister Henry Highland Garnet and the women—white and black—were attacked by the crowd. Under the threat of bodily harm, Mott asked a male escort to accompany several of the women with her, as she approached the alleged leader of the "rowdies," Captain Rynders, and grabbed his arm saying that he would escort her from the terrible scene. "Lucretia's friends were alarmed," as he quietly escorted her from the place, obviously quite emotionally disarmed.

As early as 1840, Mott and Elizabeth Cady Stanton attended the London Anti-Slavery Convention, vowing to start their own women's antislavery group since they were generally silenced by men at such gatherings at this early point of the movement.

By the summer of 1848, while visiting Seneca Falls, New York, to investigate the deteriorating plight of the Seneca Indians on reservations and the homesteads of runaway slaves, as well as visiting her friend Elizabeth Cady Stanton, Mott made the decision to organize the great Seneca Falls Convention of women. Clearly "the guiding spirit of the meeting," according to Bacon, was Lucretia Mott. She and her compatriots called "for the repeal of laws that placed women on an unequal status" and their "sacred right of elective franchise," or the right to vote. Yet remarkably, Mott was very nervous about voting rights for women initially, wondering if the governmental elective process was viable or worthy. "She was fair-minded enough to see, though, that if men were to have the right to vote, then women should also, and soon became an advocate," observed Bacon, especially following the oratory of the great Frederick Douglass, who "swayed the assembly to accept the resolution by a narrow margin."

That is not to say that there was not friction between the proponents of women's and black rights, an issue discussed by the many guests at Lucretia Mott's estate Roadside. In the end, the two sides generally reconciled with black and women's rights becoming an American reality.

The Mottses' constant activities and traveling, especially as they aged, began to take its toll. After attending a wedding in January 1868, Lucretia's husband James became very ill with pneumonia when the couple returned to their beloved Roadside, and he quietly died.

The family was devastated, with Lucretia anguishing about his absence.

Twelve years later, as 1880 approached, the once indefatigable Mott, at almost eighty-seven years old, became very ill, too, likely weakened by her chronic illnesses that included severe respiratory difficulties. "She seemed, however, to grow weaker from this time on and rarely left Roadside," wrote Bacon in *Valiant Friend*. "By early fall it was apparent that she was failing each day, gradually and without complaint." Word about the great woman's imperiled health spread throughout the region and country.

Mott died on November 11, 1880, "with all her remaining children and grandchildren about her, she peacefully breathed her last," Bacon wrote.

> [Her] *funeral was simple. Relatives and close friends gathered at Roadside for a memorial service at which several old friends spoke. Then the small coffin was taken to the Fair Hill burial grounds, where several thousand gathered silently. At the graveside only one Peace Society colleague, Henry Child, said a few words. The silence became profound. "Will no one speak?" a low voice asked. "Who can speak?" another said. "The preacher is dead."*

Jay Cooke Sets the Stage for Great Growth

Jay Cooke's presence in the community would set the stage for the grand Gilded Age in Cheltenham, perhaps America's most acclaimed neighborhood in that regard. The Old York Road Historical Society reports that Cooke actually broke ground on his Ogontz estate on the very day the war ended, April 9, 1865.

Horace Mather Lippincott, in a paper read before the Old York Road Historical Society on April 30, 1946, entitled "Jay Cooke," noted that the Ogontz mansion was constructed "on the hilltop overlooking what is now Elkins Park. Neighbors were employed, and material was procured nearby. Cooke was his own architect. He got Philadelphia artisans and furniture, built an Italian Garden, a conservatory, a ruined castle and a pool."

He further noted that the structure was "the first great residence in the State, and long a show place of the neighborhood. It stood on an eminence amid great trees, particularly the splendid chestnut trees that used to abound amongst us."

In fact, the "house cost more than $1,000,000" and had "seventy-two servants. Gas was supplied from a private plant. The house-warming was on February 14, 1867. Five hundred guests, including the President of the United States, Cabinet Ministers, Senators, diplomats, and actors were there."

Although his Jay Cooke & Company would become the leading banking house in Philadelphia and though Cooke was the first to pioneer selling bonds in small amounts directly to investors, the mogul mistakenly overexpanded his business. That assisted in the spectacular financial panic of 1873, costing many people, including Cooke, millions of dollars.

Indeed, one account of the terrible episode indicates that President Grant had been visiting Ogontz when Cooke learned of the terrible news, according to Barbara Goldsmith in her 1998 book *Other Powers*:

Jay Cooke's Ogontz mansion was called "the showplace of the nation," erected in the midst of two hundred acres near Church Road and Washington Lane. *Free Library of Philadelphia.*

Jay Cooke's mausoleum is perhaps the most prominent structure in the St. Paul's churchyard. *Kristopher Scott.*

Dinner was followed by brandy and Cooke's private brand of cigar. The two sat quietly enjoying the evening's peace. The following morning, while they consumed a breakfast of kippers and eggs, the butler placed in front of Cooke a wire from his partner Harris C. Fahnestock in New York. As soon as President Grant left, Cooke rushed to his Philadelphia office. When he arrived he was told that Fahnestock had closed the New York branch. Just two hours later, the great doors of Philadelphia's Jay Cooke & Co. on Third Street also swung shut, never to open again. Jay Cooke stood behind them weeping. The Northern pacific had failed. The panic of 1873 had begun.

Cooke departed Ogontz, selling most of its magnificent contents, and moved to the Eildon estate with his daughter and son-in-law, Charles D. Barney, who would form a new firm, C.D. Barney and Company, at which Jay Cooke held a desk.

The sanctuary of St. Paul's is dedicated to the memory of the great Jay Cooke. *Kristopher Scott.*

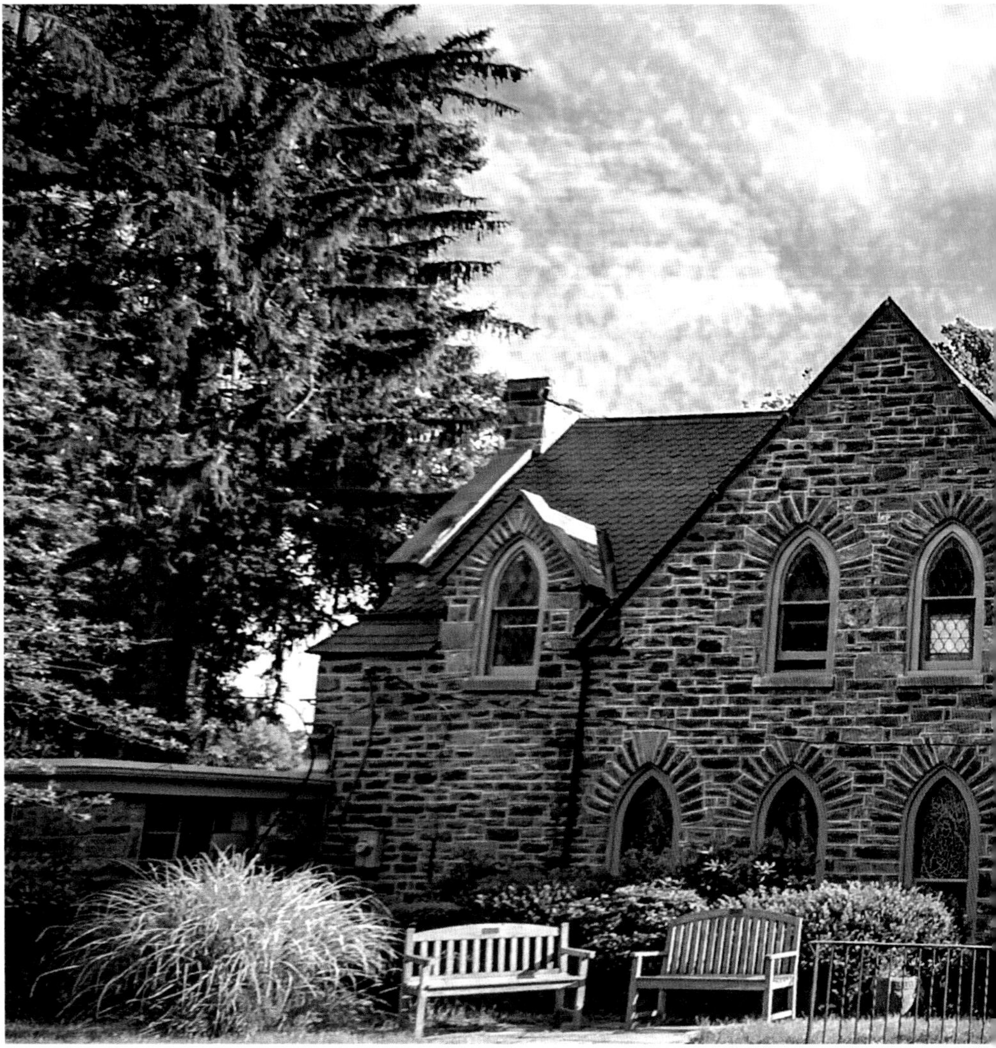

St. Paul's Episcopal Church, at Ashbourne Road and Old York Road, was designed by the architectural firm Sidney & Merry with the renowned architect Horace Trumbauer blueprinting later additions. *Kristopher Scott.*

Meanwhile, Ogontz was leased in 1883 to a "Ladies Seminary," which became the Ogontz School for Girls and at which the great trailblazing aviator Amelia Earhart attended school.

As he aged, Cooke loved to go fishing at Beach Haven, New Jersey, and at Ogontz Lodge on the Susquehanna River in Pennsylvania's Lycoming County, where he hunted bear and deer, as well as fished.

Indeed, Lippincott as "a youngster" certainly recalled Cooke "as he stopped in his one-seated buggy on so many afternoons to talk with my grandfather, Penrose Mather, who was his friend. He wore a cape cloak and white, broad-brimmed soft hat. As a child I was, of course, greatly impressed with their conversation and the gentle neighborliness of the great man."

Cooke died on February 16, 1905, at the Eildon estate. "His long life was a tribute to a robust health, an equable disposition, temperate habits, and devotion to outdoor sports," Lippincott wrote. "He had built a simple mausoleum of marble in 1867 at 'Ogontz' amid the forest" that was moved to the churchyard of nearby St. Paul's Episcopal Church, for which he had donated substantial funds during the 1860s.

St. Paul's, located on the northeast corner of Ashbourne Road and Old York Road, in fact, would become home to a number of wealthy tycoons who would soon make Cheltenham home and the church central to their Christian lives.

PART III

THE GLORIOUS GILDED AGE AND UNSPEAKABLE WEALTH

To understand the dynamic era of the Gilded Age in Cheltenham it is prudent to focus on the incredible entrepreneurial families that contributed to the township's development socially, religiously and economically, including the Wideners and Elkinses. The rags-to-riches stories of such families—who often started from very humble beginnings—symbolize the township's preeminence as a pillar of the American Gilded Age.

Indeed, the absorbing story of the Wideners is the quintessential example of super-rich families who made Cheltenham their home during the early 1900s, including the Wanamakers, Stetsons, Breyers, Steeles and many more.

The Wideners' fascinating saga in this area started on November 2, 1752, when the German immigrant Johann Cristoph Widener landed at the Philadelphia port, delivered by the ship *Phoenix* from Portsmouth. After settling in Philadelphia, he initially married Anna Kinneman but inexplicably later tied the knot with Anna Margaretha Engelhardt—records do not indicate the fate of the first marriage.

Anna and Johann had several children, including Michael, their first son, born on February 20, 1765. He married Susannah Huhn at the First Reformed Church in Philadelphia in September 1789 at the climax of the American Revolution, with the couple giving birth to daughter Susan and a son, Johannes, born on June 14, 1790. The seeds of entrepreneurship began

Likely shot in the spring based on the flowering bushes, this frontal image of Lindenhurst, Wanamaker's mansion, depicts the grandeur of such local properties that often had awnings as temperatures and the sun climbed. *Old York Road Historical Society.*

to sprout with Johannes, who developed a shipping business and became a brick maker, wrote David Whitmire for the online site Encyclopedia Titanica, in the article "The Wideners: An American Family."

Johannes married Sarah Fulmer in March 1811. The couple had three children, including Margaret and George, who operated a butcher stall on Girard Avenue. The third child was Peter Arrell Brown Widener, destined to become the patriarch tycoon of the family.

The aggressive Peter, born on November 13, 1834, attended Philadelphia public schools while apprenticing as a butcher. He saved his money to start his own shop in the Spring Garden area of the city and eventually expanded to open other stores. Meanwhile, his original stall, according to Whitmore, "became a hang out for locals who liked to discuss politics," a clue to some of P.A.B. Widener's future business activities groomed by political contacts.

In fact, Widener would soon become the political leader of the Twentieth Ward, and via "his political connections, he was awarded a government contract to supply mutton to all Union troops within a 10 mile radius of Philadelphia which earned him $50,000 in revenue," Whitmire wrote. He invested the money "in horse cars with his friend and store clerk William Elkins," who owned a produce store, and then rose to virtually monopolize that industry in Philadelphia. Widener's foresight allowed him to start one of the first meat store chains in the country.

Widener, in 1858, married Hannah Josephine Dunton. The couple had three sons, including Harry, who died about age twelve from typhoid fever; George Dunton Widener; and Joseph Early Widener. Meanwhile, a daughter, Hannah Widener, succumbed in July 1896 aboard the family yacht while sailing in Maine.

The Widener-Elkins duo soon teamed up with the Philadelphia political boss William Kemble and expanded into the street railway business. Kemble, who became president of their Philadelphia Traction Company, had a grand estate, Mary Lawn, in the Glenside area of the township. In addition to founding the Philadelphia Traction Company in 1883, they expanded their streetcar empire to such cities as New York, Chicago, Pittsburgh and Baltimore. Widener was "an organizer of the U.S. Steel Company, the American Tobacco Company, and invested in International Mercantile Marine, owner of the White Star Line and Titanic with J.P. Morgan," according to Whitmire.

William Lukens Elkins, too, had very humble beginnings, according to the November 8, 1903 *New York Times* edition that marked his death. "He came of Puritan stock. His father was a native of this city, although the family is a Virginia one," the *Times* reported.

Older than his business partner, William L. Elkins was born near Wheeling, West Virginia, on May 2, 1832. However, the first of the Elkinses to arrive in Philadelphia was William L. Elkins's grandfather, Virginia native William Elkins (born 1767), who died in Philadelphia of the plague on July 20, 1798.

It is not hard to discern how William Elkins, too, had great political abilities based on his family's impressive pedigree of politicians from West Virginia, such as U.S. senator Stephen B. Elkins, as well as via his innate shrewd wisdom. Senator Elkins (a Democrat), as a young man from Missouri, joined Union forces when the Civil War erupted, despite his father and brother fighting for the Confederacy, according to the January 5, 1911 edition of the *New York Times*.

Eventually, the senator became quite wealthy from a corporate law business, "making $50,000 a year," then marrying "a daughter of ex-Senator Harry G. Davis of West Virginia [Hallie Davis]" and solidifying massive landholdings while purchasing railroad interests; he also worked on related legislation after being elected senator and ascending to become secretary of war under President Benjamin Harrison.

William McIntire Elkins started off as a neighborhood grocer before greatly expanding the produce industry and venturing into oil and transportation with Peter A.B Widener. *Free Library of Philadelphia.*

It was obvious that Elkins, a grocer, was exceptionally driven and secure, soon co-founding the largest produce business in Philadelphia, Saybolt & Elkins. Along the way, "Mr. Elkins built the first large refrigerator in Philadelphia and upset all old-time methods by placing ice above the produce" in order to preserve it, the *Times* reported. Then he bought out his business partner.

However, the insightful Elkins had his eyes on what was then a novel industry, petroleum oil, and bought interests in western Pennsylvania, realizing that oil would be needed to produce gasoline for engines. Elkins "erected his first refining works near Lancaster Avenue and Fiftieth Street in the Twenty-fourth Ward of Philadelphia," making it "one of the first petroleum refineries in Philadelphia"—ultimately the Monument Oil Works.

The *New York Times* reported that Elkins was the first person to manufacture gasoline: "Soon afterward, in conjunction with the Monument, he operated the Park and Belmont Refineries…Here the first gasoline ever manufactured from petroleum was made," leading him to a partnership with the Standard Oil Company.

Just two years earlier, Elkins met Peter A.B. Widener via a mutual friend and associate, the politician William Baldwin. "The two men instantly became personal friends" and were popularly known as the "traction twins." Their partnership was immediately very fruitful, as both cemented ties with other influential people in politics and business.

Elkins, in fact, commissioned to design for him an incredible abode by the famed architect Horace Trumbauer. Called Elstowe Park in Chelten Hills (today part of Elkins Park, named for the tycoon), one media observer described it this way: "One of the most magnificent houses in America, a masterpiece of architecture, is the Italian Renaissance house of the traction magnate, at Elkins, in the picturesque Chelten Hills. Built of Indiana stone and granite; Caen stone and marble used inside. Its grand gallery contains 150 famous paintings" created by some of the greatest masters of all time. He even built his own railway station, Elkins Station in Ogontz, designed by renowned architects Cope and Stewardson, for $40,000.

Elkins's monumental success also ushered in marriage and children—and some heartbreak. He married Miss Maria Louise Broomall in 1858, "daughter of James Broomall of Chester County." They had two sons and two daughters. However, William L. Elkins Jr. died of apoplexy in March 1902.

For the time being, though, Widener, Elkins and Kemble became the architects of a business "syndicate" that would send shivers throughout the Northeast, including in the core of American free enterprise, New York City. The *New York Times* called the group the "strongest street passenger railroad concern in the country."

At first settling on North Broad Street at Girard Avenue in Philadelphia, Widener's increasing wealth enabled him to hire the highly esteemed architect Trumbauer to design and build Lynnewood Hall, a Georgian-style 110-room mansion on three hundred acres in Elkins Park, named after his partner William Elkins. "The grounds and elaborate gardens of the estate were designed by Jacques Greber who had redesigned the outskirts of Paris," Whitmire noted. "The estate included stables, greenhouses, a polo field and a reservoir."

Widener's association with Trumbauer would set a precedent for the future business moguls of Cheltenham and the Philadelphia metropolitan area. The architect, whose primary designer was an African American, Julian Abele, would go on to design the Wideners' Miramar estate in Newport, Rhode Island; the Harry Widener Library at Harvard University; and Ronaele Manor in Elkins Park. Indeed, the sixty-room Ronaele, the grand Tudor Revival home of Eleanor Jr. and Fitz Eugene Dixon, featured an eight-room butler's cottage, greenhouses and even an agricultural and cattle building.

However, well before the era of grandeur when Peter A.B. Widener was still expanding his butcher business, son George Dunton Widener (doomed to perish on the *Titanic* with his son Harry) was born on June 10, 1861, in Philadelphia. "He first worked in a grocery store and then joined his father's

This frontal image of Lynnewood Hall shows its majesty, not too much unlike a popular Washington, D.C. landmark, the White House. *Old York Road Historical Society.*

The son of Peter A.B. Widener, George Widener died on the *Titanic* with his son Harry. *Free Library of Philadelphia.*

business, quickly taking on the management of most of PAB's traction and streetcar business," Whitmire wrote. He became a business powerhouse in his own right, maintaining leadership and board positions with many local firms and agencies, including the Electric Storage Batter Company, the Portland Cement Company, the Land Title Bank and Trust Company and the Philadelphia Academy of the Fine Arts, just to name a few.

As the Gilded Age really took hold, George Widener married the daughter of his father's business partner, William Elkins. Eleanor Elkins and George Dunton Widener were married on November 1, 1883. They had several children, including Eleanor Jr., George Jr. and Harry Widener, destined to become a prolific book collector.

Taking up residence in the majestic Lynnewood Hall with his father and serving as senior warden at St. Paul's Episcopal Church, founded in 1861 by Jay Cooke, George Sr. was also for a time chair of Cheltenham Township's board of commissioners. Indeed, "Eleanor and their children lived at Lynnewood Hall, attended by dozens of servants," notes Whitmire.

Books, Fortune and Tragedy of the *Titanic*

An unspeakable tragedy occurred for George and Eleanor Widener, as well as their son Harry and two servants, in the spring of 1912 as they returned from Europe on the ill-fated "unsinkable" ocean liner, the *Titanic*. The Wideners, in fact, had gone to Europe shopping for their upcoming wedding trousseau for their daughter, Eleanor Jr., who was engaged to Fitz-Eugene Dixon Jr. And Harry, a prolific book collector, had reportedly sought and bought a copy of Francis Bacon's essays as the Wideners traversed the "old country." Meanwhile, George Widener, age fifty, tended to various business transactions.

As usual, they traveled in splendor, while many of their wealthy friends, including the Astors, Strauses and Guggenhems, were also destined to take up splendid quarters on the super-sized ship that was on its maiden voyage. Indeed, the Wideners even entertained such guests as the *Titanic*'s captain during a splendiferous dinner party shortly before the ship went down.

Hosting a party that Captain Edward John Smith attended only hours before the *Titanic* struck an iceberg just after 11:30 p.m. on April 14, 1912, George D. Widener and his wife Eleanor likely were quite cheerful in the vessel's fancy a la carte restaurant. As the 46,329-ton ship cruised westward from Europe toward New York City, about four hundred miles off the Newfoundland coast, these passengers dined on lobster, caviar and quail.

Just a few hours away, they would endure a legendary tragedy.

In fact, by 9:00 p.m. Captain Smith returned to the bridge of the ship where Second Officer Charles Herbert Lightoller was on the 6:00 p.m. to 10:00 p.m. watch. Officers discussed the dropping temperatures and the need to watch out for icebergs.

The ocean, though, was deceptively and bewitchingly mild, according to most observers.

After the captain departed the dinner, the ladies began to leave for the evening as their husbands enjoyed cigars and nightcaps, likely brandy. They conversed about a variety of topics, including politics and the adventures in West Virginia of Clarence Moore, who had actually interviewed Anse Hatfield, a feuding "hillbilly" in the infamous McCoy-Hatfield fight. Moore, a prolific sportsman and banker, would soon decide to help women and children into lifeboats of the sinking *Titanic*, heroically refusing to take a seat in a vessel, according to survivors.

Back in their cabin suites before or by about 11:30 p.m. the Wideners heard a crashing sound about 11:40 p.m., as Eleanor Widener told the *New York Times* in an article published on April 29, 1912, several days after the tragedy.

> *Mr. Widener and I had retired to our cabin for the night when the shock of crashing into the iceberg occurred. We thought little of it and did not leave our cabin. We must have remained there an hour before becoming fearful.*
>
> *Then Mr. Widener went to our son Harry's room and brought him to our cabin. A short time later Harry went to the deck and hurried back and told us that we must go on deck. Mr. Widener and Harry a few minutes later went on deck and aided the officers, who were then having trouble with those in the steerage. That was the last I saw of my husband or son.*

Horrifically, according to the *Times* article, Eleanor Widener actually witnessed the death of Captain Smith and a compatriot: "I went on deck and was put into a life boat. As the boat pulled away from the Titanic, I saw one of the officers shoot himself in the head and a few minutes later saw Capt. Smith jump from the bridge into the sea." The captain's body was never recovered.

The Harvard University library was named after Harry Widener following the alumnus' death aboard the *Titanic*. The Widener family contributed much capital to fund the library's construction and other related projects. *Free Library of Philadelphia.*

Peter A.B. Widener II, while a student at the St. Mark's boarding school in Massachusetts, was shocked when he learned about the *Titanic*'s sinking from classmates, according to his memoirs, *Without Drums*, published in 1940 by G.P. Putnam's Sons: "I was playing at recess just before history class one fine April day in 1912…There was spring in the air, and I thought happily of the forthcoming arrival of Uncle George. I wondered for the hundredth time what he was bringing me."

The nephew, Peter II (the son of George's brother Joseph E. Widener), would never receive that gift. One of his classmates shoved a newspaper in front of him, breaking the lad's chain of thought, as he read the shocking headline: "Titanic Sinking—1700 On Board." Peter remembered, although he felt something dreadfully wrong, that the word "Titanic" did not completely register in his mind. "The Titanic—the Titanic…Where had I heard Titanic? Uncle George! 'Why that's the ship my aunt and uncle are coming home on,' I blurted out at last, horrified recognition of the name of the ship sweeping over me."

Prayer, at that terrible moment, became Peter's primary solace: "I got down on my knees and I prayed, prayed that my uncle and my aunt, the two people I loved best in the world next to my own mother, might be spared."

Although most of the family was terrified, reportedly the great family patriarch, Peter Arrell Brown Widener, remained hopeful—at first. In her lifeboat on the Atlantic, Eleanor Elkins Widener was far from her family's

Peter Widener and his children, Joseph II and Fifi, pose for a picture. Joseph II was at school in April 1912 when he learned from a classmate that the ship *Titanic* had sunk in the North Atlantic with his uncle, George Dunton Widener, and cousin, Harry Widener, aboard. *Free Library of Philadelphia.*

stately comforts. She had to be wondering how the Widener and Elkins families were taking the terrible news of the *Titanic*'s sinking. They had to be worried about her son Harry and husband George. They also had to be concerned about the two servants, Herbert Keeping (who died with Harry and George Widener) and Amalie Henriette Gieger, Eleanor's maid.

Eleanor was exceptionally strong, even taking the oars "when exhausted seamen were on the verge of collapse," said her maid Gieger, as quoted in the book, *Sinking of the Titanic and Great Sea Disasters*, by Logan Marshall. "The girl said Mrs. Widener bravely toiled throughout the night and consoled other women who had broken down under the strain."

Hours later—relatively early on April 15—Eleanor and her fellow survivors were picked up by the RMS *Carpathia* of the Cunard Line at the direction of Captain Arthur Rostron.

Meanwhile, patriarch Peter Widener made arrangements for a private train to take his daughter-in-law from the New York City harbor where the *Carpathia* was headed. He would arrive in the train before the ship arrived.

The realization that a great tragedy had struck really set in with the family, including Peter Widener II. "My prayers were too late. In a day or two when the Carpathia came in with Titanic survivors, it brought my aunt and her maid. Uncle George and Cousin Harry had gone gallantly to their death at sea."

Despite some accounts conflicting, the finish for George Widener and his son was indeed valiant. As the ship began to sink, only hours after the Wideners' dinner with Captain Smith, Harry Widener courageously helped his mother. The online edition of Encyclopedia Titanica Passenger Biographies specifically noted: "Later that night Harry helped his mother into boat four and then stood back to await his fate, at one point he was joined by [family friend] William Ernest Carter, who advised him to try for a boat, but Harry [said], 'I'll think I'll stick to the big ship, Billy, and take a chance.'"

Philadelphia's *Evening Bulletin* of April 19, 1912, indicated that George Widener was "calm as though taking a walk on Broad Street in Philadelphia," and "stood back with Harry Elkins Widener that weaker might be rescued." A few unsubstantiated reports indicate that Harry returned to his cabin for a rare, first-edition book, Francis Bacon's *Essays*, just before the ship sank.

Somber funeral services were held one month later at St. Paul's Church—the building overflowing with floral arrangements—while family members and friends, as well as an abundance of dignitaries, paid their respects. Eleanor Widener was observed "leaning on the arm of her son, George D. Widener Jr., and dressed in deepest mourning."

Some reports indicate that George Widener and his son Harry helped women and children into lifeboats as the *Titanic* sank on April 14, 1912. *Free Library of Philadelphia.*

Tiffany windows at St. Paul's Episcopal Church were dedicated to the memory of George Dunton Widener and his son Harry Widener, who died on the *Titanic*. *Kristopher Scott.*

Even the great patriarch, Peter A.B. Widener, seemed shocked as he "walked, unattended into the church, and his somewhat shortened, halting footsteps told only too plainly the grievous effect of his son in the tragedy."

Eleanor Widener later dedicated two brilliant stained-glass Tiffany windows in memory of her husband, George, and their son, Harry—today historic fixtures in the church, originally designed by architects Sidney & Merry, with later expansions by the great Horace Trumbauer. The windows' presentation was made by Eleanor Widener Dix, the daughter of George and Eleanor Widener, who reportedly received a humongous jewel from her mother (Eleanor Sr.) reminiscent of the one featured in the recent motion picture of the *Titanic* tragedy. It was she who had married Fitz Eugene Dixon Sr. soon after her mother's *Titanic* voyage to complete her wedding trousseau.

The great matriarch, Eleanor Sr., would also donate a huge quantity of her son Harry's books and funds to Harvard University, thus creating in 1915 the school's primary library—the Harry Elkins Widener Library—the

Peter A.B. Widener was the family patriarch who started his epic career as a simple butcher to become one of America's greatest entrepreneurs. *Free Library of Philadelphia.*

cornerstone of the largest library system in the world. "The grandson [Harry] in his will left a library to Harvard University, and Mr. [Peter A.B.] Widener gave $1,000,000 to Harvard University for a building in which to keep the books," the *New York Times* reported in an obituary concerning the family patriarch, Peter A.B. Widener.

Sadly, on November 6, 1915, the venerable leader of the family, Peter I, died at his grand mansion, Lynnewood Hall, the *New York Times* reported in an extensive next-day obituary: "Mr. Widener was 80 years old, and had been in poor health for three years. Physicians said old age and deep sorrow caused by the loss of his son and his grandson in the Titanic disaster were contributing causes. Within the last week his weakened condition sapped his vitality, and he was seriously ill three days before his death." He left an estate estimated to be worth $35 million.

The Widener family after the patriarch's death and dreadful days of the *Titanic* made many notable endowments and donations worth millions of dollars, including to Widener University and the Free Library of Philadelphia, as well as passed on the paintings of masters to the National Gallery in Washington, D.C.

Many of the paintings—including Rembrandts, Van Dykes, El Grecos, Raphaels and Titians—destined for the National Gallery from a collection worth $50 million in 1940, had "hung on the walls of Lynnewood Hall… in Elkins Park, [outside of] Philadelphia," reported the October 28, 1940 edition of *Time* magazine.

Quoting Peter Widener II from his biography, *Without Drums*, the magazine seemed to herald these sagacious words:

> *The days of America's privately owned treasure houses are over. They are gone with the wind as inevitably as the great Southern plantations of before the Civil War…Today there is a general and salutary leveling of extravagance to safeguard this great heritage of ours, America…We feel that such a gift to the nation is one small step in the direction of disarming those individuals and ideologies that are foreign to the American way.*

Much of the huge Widener estate would subsequently be subdivided. A giant housing development turned apartments, Lynnewood Gardens, was

This aerial view of the Widener's estate captures its expansiveness, stretching to three hundred acres. The grounds and elaborate gardens were designed by Jacques Greber, who had redesigned the outskirts of Paris, and included stables, greenhouses, a polo field and a reservoir. *Free Library of Philadelphia.*

built at a cost of $20 million. An oval-shaped racetrack for the family's premiere horses was converted into a major thoroughfare in the sprawling complex that still exists today.

As World War II raged, the grounds of the great estate were reportedly used to train military dogs as huge parcels of land were sold off.

By 1952, the Faith Theological Seminary, a religious group, purchased the property for a mere $192,000. However, historic parts of the estate were reportedly sold off to help with mounting debt, including very valuable interior ornaments and moldings. In 2003, the property was added to the Preservation Alliance for Greater Philadelphia's 2003 list for most endangered historic properties, despite being eligible for the National Register of Historic Places.

After the Faith Theological Seminary lost the property, the thirty-four-acre site was purchased by the First Korean Church of New York. However, recent media reports indicate that the property is primarily vacant with no major noticeable repairs made, friction with the local township concerning zoning playing a possible role.

The epic 110-room Georgian mansion, designed by the renowned architect Horace Trumbauer, today is considered to be the largest surviving Gilded Age mansion in the Philadelphia region.

Edward M. Davis: An Original, Dynamic Land Developer

Edward M. Davis, the enterprising son-in-law of Lucretia Mott, was indispensable regarding the development of LaMott. Married to Mott's beloved daughter, Maria, Davis was a land developer who most affected the pattern of growth in the Cheltenham area at first, especially in LaMott.

Although he was also a merchant who operated a store at 16 South Eighth Street in Philadelphia featuring "Hats, Caps, and Straw Goods, also Full Line of Fur Goods," according to an advertisement in the July 1877 edition of the *Cheltenham Record* (published by the Cheltenham Military Academy), Davis was much more. Born in 1812, he married Lucretia Mott's daughter Maria on October 26, 1836, permanently moving to Cheltenham about 1854 on a property that he called Oak Farm, likely due to the large number of oak trees in the area.

Maria and Edward had lived adjacent to Lucretia Mott and her husband James on Ninth Street between Vine and Race Streets in Philadelphia before 1850. However, although they began to spend their summers at Oak Farm after that point, likely due to their greater involvement with the Underground Railroad following the passage of the Fugitive Slave Act in 1850, the Davises and Motts moved to Oak Farm permanently in 1854.

In addition to leasing the land to the federal government for Camp William Penn, following the North Penn Railroad arrival "to the northern suburbs in 1854, Davis formed the Chelten Hills Land Association which bought 1000 acres of farm land from neighboring Cheltenham Quakers, and then enticed many prominent Philadelphians to construct handsome country residences" in the area, according to Elaine Rothschild in her 1991 Old York Road Historical Society article "Historic LaMott."

Others who helped Davis to develop the land included Morris L. Hallowell, John W. Thomas and Frederick Fraley, who "divided" the land "and remodeled the buildings, and built new houses" that were at first primarily occupied by Irish immigrants and a small number of blacks who often worked for the rich tycoons in nearby sprawling estates. They included the likes of the investor Jay Cooke, hat maker John Stetson and John Wanamaker, the legendary department store retailer. Joining the frenzy via other routes would be such powerbrokers as the publishing magnate Cyrus H.K. Curtis and sugar tycoon William Welsh Harrison.

Davis undoubtedly had steadfast connections to some of the region's wealthiest businesspeople via his membership in the Union League of Philadelphia and became "an agent to obtain funds for them," according to Rothschild, noting that the organization provided the primary funds to establish Camp William Penn.

After the Civil War, a second wave of great entrepreneurs and the first working-class suburbanites began to settle in the Cheltenham area, with Davis developing the area that became known as LaMott. Other developments would follow, as roadways and public transportation (including horse-drawn trolleys and trains) expanded into the area, leading to such communities as Ashbourne, developed by Richard J. Dobbins, who lived in his grand estate Ellerslie that was located near Old York and Ashbourne Roads, according to the Old York Road Historical Society. Other turn-of-the-century communities became known as Wyncote, Glenside and Ogontz Park (today Elkins Park). Yet before those areas would fully develop, the palatial homes of the rich and famous would take root before the township morphed into a semblance of its modern form.

Cyrus H.K. Curtis and the Making of a Publishing Dynasty

Born in 1850 in Portland, Maine, about ten years before the Civil War, Cyrus H.K. Curtis was destined to found one of the greatest publishing empires in the world and settle in Cheltenham, where he lived on his sprawling estate, Lyndon, on the southeast corner of Greenwood Avenue and Church Road.

The original structure was built in 1866 by Abraham Barker, a powerful finance banker whose son Wharton unsuccessfully ran for president against William McKinley as a Populist candidate in 1890. However, due to financial misfortunes in 1890, Barker "had to relinquish his dream house," according to Elaine Rothschild's 1979 *Old York Road Historical Society Bulletin* article "The Man Behind Cheltenham's Curtis Arboretum." After first renting the property in 1891, Curtis later bought it in 1895 when he hired architect William Lloyd Baily to design a new $2 million Renaissance Revival estate, according to the Old York Road Historical Society, on land that eventually stretched to 170 acres.

Landscaping, according to a Pennsylvania historical marker, was designed by the renowned architect Frederick Law Olmsted on grounds that today serve as a very attractive forty-seven-acre arboretum for the township, with memorial tributes to the many war veterans of Cheltenham, including World War II hero Arnold Snyder, who fought at the Battle of the Bulge and Normandy's Omaha Beach. The property became so well known that part of the nation's Centennial Exhibition featured Alexander Graham Bell demonstrating an early version of the telephone in June 1876.

The estate was then acquired by Curtis who, like others of this time period, had risen from meager origins to become wealthy through "hard work, perseverance, ingenuity, native intelligence, boundless energy, and little income tax," noted Rothschild.

In fact, at sixteen Curtis left high school after just his first year when the family home was destroyed in the Great Fire of Portland in 1866; he began to sell the Portland-based *Courier*, *Portland Press* and *Portland Argus* newspapers to Civil War soldiers, a booming business in those days. He eventually held a number of newspaper and advertising positions and even started one in Portland, the *Young American*, before establishing in Boston a weekly called the *People's Ledger* in 1872 after the manufacturing plant of the Portland paper was destroyed by fire.

Several years later, he moved to Philadelphia, drawn by the less expensive printing costs. In Philly he initiated another periodical, *Tribune and Farmer*, before

George Horace Lorimer was the primary editor in 1898 of the *Saturday Evening Post*, owned by Cyrus Curtis. Lorimer hired incredible illustrators, including the great Norman Rockwell, causing the circulation to skyrocket. *Free Library of Philadelphia.*

in 1897 purchasing for just $1,000 the *Saturday Evening Post*, a publication with great growth potential. He also founded the Curtis Publishing Company.

With his wife, Louisa Knapp, he co-founded *Ladies' Home Journal*, which was developed from a one-page column she had written, "Women at Home," for *Tribune and Farmer.* The women's magazine by the end of the nineteenth century had a press run of five million, spurred by the terrific editorship of Edward Bok. It wasn't long before Curtis ventured into the newspaper business, purchasing the *Philadelphia Public Ledger*, but he lost money and decided to focus more on magazines.

After investing much of his own money in the *Saturday Evening Post* and hiring the greatly respected George Horace Lorimer as the primary editor in 1898, the publication's circulation exploded. Lorimer, in turn, hired very sharp editors and such incredible illustrators as Norman Rockwell. He eventually served as vice-president, president and chairman of the Curtis Publishing Company, also building an estate (Belgrame) that is today the Ancillae Assumpta Academy (a half-mile west of Curtis's Lyndon), one of the top private schools in the United States.

Meanwhile, Curtis became very health-conscious after failing "a physical examination for life insurance," according to Rothschild. "His whole lifestyle and temperament were carefully changed to improve his health." At his Wyncote estate he had built "a nine-hole golf course, rode horseback, walked rather than rode, traveled to Europe, and, eventually acquired a series of yachts until he owned the largest pleasure-yacht in the United

Curtis Hall of the Cyrus Curtis estate was originally the music conservatory for the sprawling estate. Today it serves as a meeting place for government meetings and can be booked for private affairs, including weddings. *Old York Road Historical Society.*

States [*Lyndonia*]." For his employees he built the Curtis Country Club, which opened in 1916 on the Tookany Creek Parkway near Front Street and Ashmead Road on more than 150 acres and featured sports fields, a swimming pool, tennis courts and, of course, a clubhouse. In 1947, the property became the Melrose Country Club.

Partially named "Hermann Kotzschmar" for a gifted Portland musician of German ancestry, Curtis's "leisure time was spent at his organ which he replaced a few times, first installing it in the main part of his house and then in the music room," the only remaining building of his estate that exists today as a meeting place for township government groups and private events, including for weddings and so forth.

Although his publishing empire eventually collapsed due to a variety of reasons, including the rising cost of paper, Curtis became one of the wealthiest Americans of all time. He donated millions of dollars to the likes of the Franklin Institute, the University of Pennsylvania and other organizations.

Curtis suffered a heart attack during the summer of 1932 while aboard his prized yacht *Lyndonia* and died on June 7, 1933, at age eighty-two.

His daughter, Mary Louise Curtis Bok, founded the Curtis Institute of Music, dedicating it to her father in 1924. In 1943, she married violinist Efrem

Zimbalist, the director of the institute. A child and grandchild of Zimbalist and his former late wife, Alma Gluck (the renowned soprano), became well-known actors Efrem Zimbalist Jr. (son) and granddaughter Stephanie Zimbalist.

HENRY W. BREYER'S SWEET ICE CREAM KINGDOM

Born the same year as Cyrus Curtis, in 1850, Henry W. Breyer Sr. as a young man helped to expand the family's ice cream business from a small store in the Frankford section of Philadelphia to two full-fledged factories in Philadelphia following the death of his father, William A. Breyer.

He actually took the helm of the company in 1907 following the death of his co-partner brother, Frederick, and his widowed mother Louisa's retirement from the business.

Destined to make Cheltenham his home, Henry Breyer was responsible for the company's "pledge of purity" guarantee that the delectable treat had no artificial ingredients. The company grew dramatically and sales soared, largely due to his incredible organizational skills and the product's outright tastiness.

In 1915, Breyer constructed a very large Colonial Revival–style stone dwelling called Haredith (designed by architects Koelle, Speth & Co. and named, in part, to honor his wife Edith) in Cheltenham along Old York Road, several blocks above Church Road. Edith Breyer made sure that the dwelling always had very fine and up-to-date furnishings, redesigning its interior repeatedly. Many paintings by the world's great masters adorned the walls as she showed off exquisite Chippendale items and other prized ornaments.

"As the 1920s came to a close, Breyer was still selling more ice cream than any other firm in the United States," according to an online company profile.

The savvy businessman and financier built additional factories in New York and New Jersey before turning the business over to his son. Breyer became an investment broker, giving $10 million to family and long-serving employees upon his death in 1936.

The property, which today serves as the primary administrative building of the township with the adjacent police department headquartered on the grounds, sits on a portion of the historic Cheltenham Flour Mill property that was operated by the Shoemaker family. Placed on the National Register of Historic Places, the property was located quite near to such estates as the Wanamakers (of retail department store fame), with some reports indicating

The property, which today serves as the primary administrative building of the township with the adjacent police department headquartered on the grounds, was formerly the mansion of Henry Breyer of Breyer's Ice Cream fame. *Old York Road Historical Society.*

that Breyer purchased that property on about eighty acres for approximately $1 million in 1929. Much of that land was eventually signed over to the Boy Scouts of America and used for campgrounds.

The great entrepreneur died at age fifty-seven of a heart attack on March 5, 1936. A son, Henry W. Breyer Jr., was likely living at the home in 1936, but by 1949 Edith was probably living at the house alone.

After the property was sold to the nearby Beth Sholom Congregation, Cheltenham Township purchased it in April 1956.

John Wanamaker, the Ultimate Retailer and Deal Maker

John Nelson Wanamaker, who built his grand estate called Lindenhurst in Cheltenham, was born on July 11, 1838, and became the nation's premier retailer, as well as received an appointment as U.S. postmaster by President

John Wanamaker's Lindenhurst mansion in Cheltenham, on Old York Road just below Washington Lane, was constructed on a 108-acre site and called Lindenhurst due to the vast amount of Linden trees in the area. *Free Library of Philadelphia.*

Benjamin Harrison. He was also considered by some experts to be the father of modern advertising.

Banking on the motto "One price and goods returnable," Wanamaker—after marrying Mary Erringer Brown in 1860—opened his first store, Oak Hall, in 1861 at the dawn of the Civil War. The building was erected near the former site of President George Washington's presidential home in which the commander in chief kept nine enslaved Africans at Sixth and Market Streets, where a memorial will be erected in their honor. Business soared during the Civil War, making Wanamaker by most accounts the largest clothing retailer in the country. By 1875, he had substantially expanded his enterprises by opening a very large store that was converted from an abandoned railroad depot. He called it John Wanamaker & Co., Philadelphia's first department store.

By 1877, Wanamaker pioneered the concept of adding "departments" under the same roof, thus cleverly developing a great marketing concept that attracted hordes of buyers. "He had many special touches in his stores, including Ford dealerships, the world's largest organ which was featured in the atrium, and a telegraph receiving station on the roof, which was the first to receive word that the Titanic had sunk," notes his online biography entry. His enterprise also featured the first in-house restaurants.

The great retailer had a reputation for treating employees extremely well. They received modern benefits only being introduced at the time, including college tuition incentives or payments, life insurance, a pension, healthcare and even vacation time. However, labor activists labeled him as being extremely anti-union, charging that he fired employees in 1887 after they joined a labor group, the Knights of Labor.

As the turn of the century approached, Wanamaker opened stores in New York, London and Paris, gaining a reputation as being fair to African Americans and Native Americans.

Although Wanamaker owned homes in many parts of the world—from Philadelphia (an English manor–style dwelling on Walnut Street) to London and Paris—his beloved residence was Lindenhurst in Cheltenham, on Old York Road, just below Washington Lane. Constructed on a 108-acre site, it was called Lindenhurst when Wanamaker had it constructed at just age thirty likely due to the vast number of Linden trees in the area. "The house was built in the Queen Anne style, complete with luxurious amenities that included a reflecting pool, conservatories, stables, an artificial lake, a two-story playhouse for Wanamaker's children, a billiard room, and a bowling alley," according to writer-historian Charlene Mires of Villanova University.

John Wanamaker contributed funds for construction at St. Paul's Episcopal Church, as well as established a pioneering department store chain that developed many novel retail concepts that are still practiced today. *Free Library of Philadelphia.*

Although the residence had to be reconstructed after a 1907 fire, Wanamaker received such visitors there as U.S. president Benjamin Harrison, who planted a small oak tree on the property, "symbolic of Oak Hall," the legendary retailer's first store.

Furthermore, nearby, Wanamaker even built his own railway station, Chelten Hills, near the borough of Jenkintown, making it easier for commutes to and from work in Philadelphia and beyond.

Wanamaker's estate when he died in 1922 was valued at about $35 million, with Philadelphia mayor J. Hampton Moore calling him "the world's most distinguished merchant," according to Mires.

William Welsh Harrison's Magnificent Sugar Empire

Born in 1850, similar to other Cheltenham tycoons, William Welsh Harrison made the bulk of his money as a sugar baron, using some of his immense capital to contract the designing and building of a grand castle for his residence that today serves as an administration building for the historic Arcadia University in Glenside.

Architect Horace Trumbauer was not quite twenty-five years old when he was commissioned by Harrison after a mansion (Rosedale Hall) that he had purchased in the spring of 1881 from J. Thomas Audenreid was destroyed in a January 1893 fire. Trumbauer was a natural pick because Harrison had been pleased with his previous expansion of Rosedale Hall that included enlarging the primary house and adding a gatehouse, as well as redesigned stables.

Arcadia University's website notes that "[b]y March [1893] the architect had completed his plans for a grandiose structure based on Alnwick Castle, the medieval seat of the Dukes of Northumberland in England," reflective of Harrison's ancestry—he had written a genealogy book about how his roots preceded twelfth-century England. "The new residence…would be inspired by Alnwick, but not directly copied from it. Conveniences of the most modern kind were to be provided, including electricity."

The gray stone for the massive building was extracted from a quarry in nearby Chestnut Hill, "modeled on a Northumbrian castle, featuring numerous large and small turrets and chimneys" with the interior having intricate "mahogany carvings and paneling, cairn stone mantlepieces, ornate gold leaf light fixtures, beveled Belgian glass, and a large, intact, in-situ collection of American-made Baumgarten tapestry," notes a website dedicated to documenting the architecture of American universities, the Historic Campus Architecture Project, sponsored by the Council of Independent Colleges.

The central great hall in the building reflects Trumbauer's interest in the French Renaissance, featuring mantles carved from stone, "interpretations of a huge Renaissance mantle in the Salle des Gardes of the Francis I wing of the royal Chateau of Blois."

The main building, today called Grey Towers due to the building's stone color, has the coat of arms of Harrison's father, George Leib Harrison, a graduate of Harvard University and attorney who co-established and later managed with his three sons (William W. Harrison, Alfred Craven Harrison and Charles Custis Harrison) the Franklin Sugar Refinery. The sons erected a memorial to their grandfather (George's father), John Harrison, at the University of Pennsylvania because he was deemed to be America's first industrial chemist.

Established in 1864 by Harrison, Havemeyer & Co. "on the site of the first sugar refinery in the United States," Franklin Sugar in 1875 produced

120 million pounds of sugar. "There is no larger or better-equipped refinery in the world," noted John Thomas Scharf and Thompson Westcott's book *History of Philadelphia, 1609–1884*, published in 1884.

The growth, harvesting and manufacturing of sugar cane during the slavery era led to the enslavement of countless Africans and African Americans; 80 percent of the sugar company's employees were said to be black. Paradoxically, Harrison's paternal great-grandfather, a Quaker named Thomas Harrison, was an ardent antislavery abolitionist during the mid-1700s who married Sarah Richards, destined to become a celebrated Quaker preacher.

Meanwhile, the relationship between Harrison and his wife, Bessie, was said to be acrimonious at certain points, with oral history or legend indicating that they even lived in separate wings of their palatial home. There were even allegations that Harrison kept a mistress at a residence along the Jersey shore. The 1900 U.S. census indicates that the couple was married at that point twenty-one years and had two young adults (their children) living with them, Geraldine D. Harrison and William W. Harrison Jr., a future benefactor of Abington Memorial Hospital.

Designated a National Historic Landmark in 1985, the sprawling estate and "the castle," as it is sometimes called today, was bought by what was then known as Beaver College in 1928, one year after Welsh's death. Beaver College became Arcadia University and changed its name in 2001, more than 150 years following its western Pennsylvania origins in 1853 as the Beaver Female Seminary in Beaver, Pennsylvania, northwest of Pittsburgh. After relocating to nearby Jenkintown in 1925, along the way becoming temporarily coeducational before permanently keeping that status in 1972, Arcadia University is today a premiere liberal arts institution with an extensive overseas educational curriculum.

John B. Stetson: Supreme Hat Maker

Born on May 5, 1830, in Orange, New Jersey, John Batterson Stetson would also make Cheltenham his residence in a grand mansion called Idro (in Russian meaning "cool and pleasant") by inventing and manufacturing the ever popular cowboy hat, greatly expanding his hat-making empire just after the Civil War, similar to other Gilded Age moguls in the area.

Although he was the seventh of twelve children, Stetson's father, a hat-maker or batter, taught him the art of creating such head domes despite his son's early illness from tuberculosis. One doctor, according to historical sources, believed that his prognosis was poor and predicted that Stetson would die. And although some historical accounts indicate that Stetson then decided to explore the American West before his demise, other sources indicate that he journeyed there for the fresh air and clean environs to improve his health.

However, the company's website today notes that Stetson "headed west prepared to make his fortune. But what he wasn't prepared for was the wet and the cold that followed him every step of the way. So, in 1865, Stetson set out to make the hat that could tame the American West. And as they say, the rest is history."

In fact, Stetson was enthralled with the culture of the West, carefully observing cowboys and their lifestyles as the Civil War raged in the North and South. The practical-minded and observant young man realized that on the open plains such ranch and range workers needed better hats than animal-skin hats laced with fur. They needed something that could help shield them from the sun but at the same time be waterproof and relatively lightweight. He envisioned the hat even being used as a vessel to hold water to quench thirst and to flap up a breeze on the hot plains.

"In 1865, with $100, John B. Stetson rented a small room, bought the tools he needed, bought $10 worth of fur and the John B. Stetson Hat Company was born," notes the firm's online history. "A year later the 'Hat of the West' or the now famous 'Boss of the Plains' hat was born."

Born on May 5, 1830, in Orange, New Jersey, John Batterson Stetson made his substantial fortune by inventing and manufacturing the ever popular cowboy hat. *Free Library of Philadelphia.*

Using the skills that he acquired from his father, Stetson designed the cowboy hat, partially patterned off of the Mexican sombreros of the period. The product became immensely popular and revolutionized the industry as Stetson expanded into making fedoras and women's hats.

Lois H. Hirsch, in her online compilation of Stetson's biography for Cheltenham Township, focused on the company's initial years in Philadelphia, where Stetson opened his first shop:

> *Young John returned East in 1865, settled in Philadelphia and opened a hat repair business in a one-room shop on the northeast corner of 7th and Callowhill Streets. In a short time his talent for trimming led him to manufacturing hats. Insisting on a policy of "none but that of sterling quality," his business improved so rapidly that he needed larger quarters in just over a year. He moved his business to 4th Street above Chestnut and in no time his hats were being sold in most of the retail establishments in Philadelphia.*

A variety of historical sources, including Hirsch's account, provide an intriguing saga of a great American entrepreneur. For instance, Stetson relied on a brigade of "traveling salesmen" by 1869 and soon established himself on a twelve-acre northeast Philly campus with sophisticated buildings

Legendary hat maker John B. Stetson would also make Cheltenham his residence in a grand mansion called Idro (in Russian meaning "cool and pleasant"). *Free Library of Philadelphia.*

dedicated to manufacturing, as well as healthcare and community support programs for workers and local residents. He even constructed a school, a library and a "free" hospital, likely spurred by the bouts with tuberculosis that plagued him with a persistent cough most of his life. And if that wasn't enough, according to Hirsch, he contracted a 111-piece orchestra that provided regular musical entertainment. He even set up accommodations for employees to practice religion since he was said to be a very pious man and a devout Baptist.

It goes without saying that his employees received excellent pay and benefits, including "below-market rate loans," similar to modern credit unions.

Although he built a grand home in DeLand, Florida, Stetson's summer quarters was Cheltenham's Idro, which was located near what is today Juniper Avenue in the Ashbourne section of Elkins Park off of the west side of Old York Road. Built on land purchased from R.J. Dobbins during the late 1880s of local stone, the house had its own power plant for electricity and steam, as well as a conservatory and other accoutrements. The mansion, built in the French chateau style on fifteen acres, contained a huge gallery, a music room and a gymnasium, according to the Old York Road Historical Society.

Furthermore, Stetson, who married several times and whose son John Jr. became an ambassador to Poland, was intrigued by plant life and built enormous greenhouses at Idro and at his Florida estate, where he had extensive orange groves.

Called "America's foremost hat manufacturer," Stetson's company became one of the largest and most modern in the world as he became phenomenally wealthy. Before his death in 1906, the patriotic Stetson had been the benefactor of many causes and institutions, which included establishing a military company and armory and building grammar and high schools, as well as donating a massive amount of capital to build Temple (Philadelphia) and Stetson (Florida) Universities. He also helped to establish the YMCA in Philadelphia.

As the Gilded Age of Cheltenham's tycoons continued but eventually wound down—and Stetson's widow (third wife) Sarah Elizabeth married the famous sculptor Count of Santa Eulalia (or Alexio de Queiroz Riderio de Sotto) of Portugal in 1908—the area's large estates began to be subdivided, making way for the township's current neighborhoods. Today, despite many of the properties being razed, such as Stetson's Idro, enough remain to remind us of yesterday's incredible grandeur.

Joseph M. Steele: A Builder's Dynasty

Born in 1865, Joseph M. Steele was a dominant industrial and commercial builder who constructed Philadelphia's historic Shibe Park, his "most famous structure," according to local historian and architect Leon Clemmer, whose mother Maizie was the daughter of Joseph Steele.

With Scotch-Irish roots, several "generations of the Steele family worked together to build the largest and most successful design-build firm that Philadelphia and Toronto, Canada have ever known," noted Clemmer, the architect of the Glenside Library and many other buildings in the region and the man who also worked on the restoration of Philadelphia's historic Carpenter's Hall, where the first Continental Congress met in 1774.

"Grandfather William Steele arrived in Philadelphia from Ulster in 1853 at the age of twelve years," Clemmer wrote in his 1984 *Old York Road Historical Society Bulletin* article "The Steeles of Caversham Mansion and Ballanreas, Cheltenham, PA." "In 1864 he married Ellen Ann Blair of Ballanreas, Ireland and they settled in the Kensington section of Philadelphia." Clemmer's enterprising grandfather was a carpenter and builder quite active in north Philadelphia. Joseph was the couple's first son. Then came John, Rachael, Esther, Andrew, William and Edward.

Although Joseph studied briefly at Central High School, as well at the Spring Garden Institute and Peirce Business School, he became associated with the family firm, first known as "William Steele and J.M. Steele, Carpenters" but by "1886 they were 'William Steele and Son, Carpenters and Builders.'" Edward, another son, "joined the firm after graduation from Cornell University as a Mechanical Engineer in 1906."

In 1904, Joseph Steele—later a trustee of Drexel and Beaver College (today Arcadia University)—bought Caversham Mansion sitting on sixteen acres of land near the intersection of Washington Lane and Ashbourne Road in Chelten Hills. Joseph added electricity and a telephone, remembered Clemmer, whose mother Maizie would marry Dr. Leon Clemmer of Oak Lane in 1920; Dr. Clemmer was the eventual head of the Obstetrics and Gynecology Department at Hahnemann Hospital.

A devout Christian who at one point was the president of the Philadelphia YMCA and a board member of the Union League of Philadelphia, Joseph Steele funded many early Christian events and projects, as well as befriended the great retailer John Wanamaker, who lived nearby. The family attended the Fourth Covenanters Church, although family guests often attended Wanamaker's nearby St. Paul's Episcopal Church in Elkins Park.

In fact, as the Roaring Twenties rolled in, the Steele family's firm occupied "its own building at 15th and Arch Streets" in Philadelphia and by 1926 "was at its zenith," according to Clemmer, constructing some of the largest buildings in the city, on the U.S. East Coast and in eastern Canada. The firm, after expanding in the materials business, even supplied much of the concrete used to build Philadelphia's subway infrastructure.

Following Joseph's "father's [William] death in 1908, Joseph built a home on his own property for his mother and his sister Esther," named Ballanreas for the town in Ireland from which his mother had come to America. Clemmer described Ballanreas as a "Tudor with a stone base, half timber and slate roof."

Joseph Steele died in 1957 at the ripe age of ninety-three, leaving behind a very rich legacy.

PART IV

HISTORIC NEIGHBORHOODS WITH MATCHLESS ARCHITECTURE

WYNCOTE'S PROUD HISTORY AND ARCHITECT HORACE TRUMBAUER

The community of Wyncote, including Cedarbrook, is composed of 108 acres with buildings that were constructed between 1885 and 1915 by some of the most skilled architects of the period, including Horace Trumbauer and probably his chief designer, Julian Abele, despite contemporary debates concerning the amount of Abele's contributions.

Deemed in October 1986 as the "Wyncote Historic District"—a beautiful Victorian neighborhood west of the Jenkintown railroad station—it was also listed on the National Register of Historic Places.

Spurred by the development of the growing railway lines, starting in 1885 growth "progressed rapidly over the next thirty years, and then ceased, leaving a quiet, residential and affluent suburban neighborhood," according to Doreen L. Foust's 1987 article for the *Old York Road Historical Society Bulletin*, "Wyncote's Historic District."

Indeed, very "early development took place on the steep hills close to the railroad line, a section that remains today the most densely built part of the district," says Foust. "It was known as 'Wyncote Village' well into the twentieth century."

A truck driver of J. Howard Hay Painting truck, based in Wyncote, passes by the Montgomery County Ice and Cold Storage Company. The ice firm was situated on Glenside Avenue with the painting enterprise on Greenwood Avenue, east of Fernwood Avenue, according to the Old York Road Historical Society. *Old York Road Historical Society.*

Before that point, in addition to the aforementioned Widener, Elkins, Curtis, Wannamaker and Cooke families building grand estates in Wyncote, others such as the wealthy banker Abraham Barker also settled in the area, Foust noted, adding that such "Philadelphians bought the first homes in Wyncote both for their own use and for summer rentals."

By 1915 the district's houses had become primarily year-round residences for wealthy families. Soon, at least a half-dozen "builders, including four who already lived in Wyncote, constructed handsome houses to appeal to upper-income residents," including Willis P. Hazard and Martin Luther Kohler. As the turn of the century approached, by 1898 "Wyncote resident William E. Weber completed development in the village." Furthermore, along the way, Bradley Redfield and Edwin Tyson, a local merchant, also developed and/or subdivided land in Wyncote. "By 1915 the great majority of lots were sold and most of the extant houses were constructed," Foust wrote. Such developers tried to ensure that "Wyncote would remain an exclusive community" by making strict "deed requirements with minimum building costs and lot sizes that restricted home ownership to wealthier individuals."

Wyncote by World War I, according to Foust, had "become a stable, affluent, and rather isolated community." She noted that residents included owners of the Philadelphia area's top businesses and companies and that many were "lawyers, doctors, dentists, educators and financiers."

Artistic types also made Wyncote home, including "Christopher Morley who humorously satirized Wyncote under the pseudonym 'Marathon' in his collection of essays in *Mince Pie* published in 1919."

The homes were built in a variety of ways with diverse material. Stone houses were built on Greenwood Avenue during the 1870s, and "modest frame houses" were built on Woodland Road. Other "larger dwellings in the fashionable Queen Anne style" with ample bays and "a great variety of porches" were built. "Wyncote had a liking for towers—square, round or polygonal—all punctuating the architectural landscape of this picturesque community." Most of the Queen Anne homes were "built of Wissahickon schist stone, often quarried within the district."

Furthermore, revival styles were used in the designs of Angus S. Wade on homes in the 100 block of Fernbrook Avenue, with a Tudor Revival residence being featured in the March 1894 "Builder's Edition" of *Scientific American*, Foust noted. In fact, the Tudor style, "with its stucco and timberwork, is well expressed in the All Hallows Episcopal Church rectory" on Bent Road, she remarked.

Old Hallows, at 262 Bent Road, has roots to 1891, when worshippers at the nearby Our Saviour of Jenkintown asked that their rector help in organizing a mission and church school in Wyncote. By 1892, a wood-frame chapel was constructed, and just a few years later in 1896 the cornerstone of the current church, designed in the English Gothic style by the eminent architect Frank Furness, was laid. Local developer Martin Luther Kohler, with the financial assistance of W.W. Frazier, also helped to start the church. And the great publishing tycoon Cyrus Curtis, who lived nearby off Church Road and Greenwood Avenue, was an original member of the congregation and eventually paid off the mortgage, according to the church history. Several stained-glass windows were created by Tiffany and Company of New York, according to Foust.

Nearby, "Calvary Presbyterian was designed by the architectural firm of Dull and Peterson of Philadelphia," Foust noted, also mentioning Calvary's English Gothic style. "This church features an auditorium-like central space and an adjacent square, castellated tower which stands as a beacon atop the church hill." The church's inception stems to Easter

The Notre Dame High School for girls was located on the north side of Church Road at the corner of Greenwood Avenue, housed in a mansion originally built in 1925 by Cyrus Curtis for his stepdaughter and her husband, John C. Martin. After Ritter Finance bought the building in 1955 and occupied it, the Reconstructionist Rabbinical College became established there in 1982. *Old York Road Historical Society.*

Sunday, March 29, 1891, when the "Wyncote Mission...[started] by members of Grace Church, Jenkintown, held its first service in the small chapel that stood at the corner of Greenwood and Fernbrook Avenues." Calvary Presbyterian Church was then organized on May 20, 1892, according to the church history. Both churches were formally dedicated in 1898.

Indicative of the significant historical Jewish presence in Cheltenham, the Reconstructionist Rabbinical College at the corner of Greenwood Avenue and Church Road, was founded in 1968 by the founder of the Reconstructionist movement, Mordecai Kaplan. Originally based in brownstone buildings on North Broad Street in Philadelphia, the seminary relocated in 1982 to the Georgian-style mansion in Wyncote built in 1924 by Horace Trumbauer for Cyrus Curtis's stepdaughter and husband, John C. Martin. When the Martins moved by 1947, the structure was occupied by the Notre Dame High School for girls for

Workers at Benson Iron Works on Greenwood Avenue had a great reputation for quality work. Their work, including winding stairways, appeared in many area local residences. *Old York Road Historical Society.*

almost one decade before being bought by the Ritter Finance Company for its headquarters. Today, the college has a working relationship with the nearby Gratz College, which is also dedicated to educating those of Jewish heritage.

One of the most noteworthy Horace Trumbauer designs was the Jenkintown-Wyncote railroad station, designed in 1932 in the Tudor Revival style, Foust points out, adjacent to the "five-acre Ralph Morgan Park, through which the Tookany Creek flows." There's also a "matching, small waiting room," designed by Trumbauer, "across the tracks from the main station. A small baggage room, which was constructed at the same time as an earlier station survives on the east side of the tracks."

In the Cedarbrook area of Wyncote, a sprawling golf course at the Cedarbrook Country Club was built in 1965, designed by the former great golf professional George Fazio, adjacent to a towering apartment complex that is today called the Towers of Wyncote.

Area Contributions of the Black Architect Julian Abele

Although Trumbauer is credited with designing many outstanding buildings in Wyncote, his chief designer after 1909 was an African American, Julian Abele, who likely designed or contributed to the blueprint drawings of a wide range of buildings, including some in Wyncote.

Abele also designed or had major input in designing the Philadelphia Museum of Art, the main branch of the Free Library of Philadelphia and Harvard's Widener Memorial Library. Abele, a graduate of the historic Institute for Colored Youth in Philadelphia that later became the historically black college Cheyney University, was the first black architecture graduate of the University of Pennsylvania's architecture department in 1902. Trumbauer reportedly also sent Abele to France to study architecture, likely at the École des Beaux-Arts in Paris, allowing him to contribute to the design of some of the great mansions of Wyncote and elsewhere, despite some observers insisting that his contributions were limited.

Today, although originally occupied primarily by wealthy whites, Wyncote is a diverse community of various ethnic groups, including Protestant European-Americans, Jews, blacks from throughout the African Diaspora and Asians, often from Korean peninsula.

There are also many other Cheltenham communities with historic and significant architectural attributes.

Children and their parents fill the lawn of Trinity Chapel in Old Cheltenham, located on the northeast corner of Central and Laurel Avenues. The Episcopal congregation met there starting in 1906 when the structure was built. Eventually moving to a new facility at Central and Cottman Avenues, the structure became home for a Lutheran congregation through 1955. *Old York Road Historical Society.*

Cheltenham Village, Shoemakertown and Rowland Park

The great writer and antislavery abolitionist Harriet Beecher Stowe reportedly lived in the borders of the township's Cheltenham Village on Elm Avenue when she wrote her novel *Uncle Tom's Cabin* (published 1852), which many historians believe was the greatest literary influence on feelings of Northern sympathy for those trapped in slavery. The areas of Cheltenham Village and Rowland Park on the eastern end of the township actually have roots to the old mills that developed there since European colonists arrived during the late 1600s, including Thomas Rowland, who operated Thomas Rowland & Sons Shovel Works. The millworkers at such enterprises began to settle in the area as various enterprises and institutions developed to support them. Rowland, in fact, had an African American "servant," Eliza Larkin, with whom he attended the nearby

Cheltenham United Methodist Church (established circa 1816). Both were reportedly buried in the nearby church cemetery. Although single homes had been constructed in the area since the mid- to late 1700s, twin dwellings were built starting in the 1920s with more single dwellings developed during the 1930s up to the 1960s.

Laverock

The community of mostly single, elegant homes in the southwest area of Cheltenham developed around attorney John Clark Sims's estate, which was constructed during the early 1890s. Serving as the secretary and vice-president of the Pennsylvania Railroad, Sims (born 1845) adored the property that was simply initially known as the Sims estate. This is before the name Laverock Hill was adopted after it was purchased by financier and socialite Isaac T. Starr. Starr reportedly hired the acclaimed New York architect Charles A. Platt and the well-known landscape designer Ellen Biddle Shipman to refurbish the residence and garden. Working on the property from 1915 to 1918, Platt created a handsome Georgian mansion surrounded by service buildings, a barn and a greenhouse encircled by quaint red brick walls. Although the initial development of Laverock started during the 1920s, not many homes were built after the Depression of the 1930s. However, during the 1950s and 1960s, split-level homes were built amid the older stone residences and an abundance of large black oak trees. A multicultural community today, Laverock's citizens have been fighting fiercely to preserve historical elements of the area, including Laverock Hill.

Elkins Park (Ogontz Park), Ashbourne and Melrose Park

Named for the great entrepreneur William McIntire Elkins, Elkins Park (earlier known as Ogontz Park for Jay Cooke's estate) is home to the only synagogue ever designed by the legendary architect Frank Lloyd Wright (Beth Sholom Synagogue). Meaning the "House of Peace," Wright completed in 1959 the architectural marvel that symbolizes "the great mountain which Moses climbed to receive the Ten Commandments from God," according to a 1989 article written by Thuy Nguyen for the *Old York Road Historical Society Bulletin*. The Melrose Park section of Elkins Park is also the home of Gratz College, the oldest such institution of Jewish studies in the western hemisphere, with roots to the Hebrew Education Society of Philadelphia, founded in 1849 by Rebecca Gratz and Isaac Leeser. In nearby Ashbourne stood the estate of Richard J. Dobbins (Ellerslie), a local architect and builder, whose property was eventually demolished but today is the site of Adath Jeshurun and the Mandell Education Campus of the Federation of Jewish Agencies of Philadelphia.

The home of Richard Wall (circa 1682), which is said to be "the oldest house in Pennsylvania which has had continuous family residence," and the historic abode of Tobias Leech are located within the perimeter of Elkins Park. Current or former residents of Elkins Park include Benjamin Netanyahu, the prime minister of Israel; Ralph J. Roberts (co-founder of Comcast); Jeffrey Solow, a renowned virtuoso cellist; and Peter A.B. Widener, the transportation dynasty partner of William Elkins. Edgar Lee Masters, a renowned poet and writer, died in a Melrose Park nursing home in 1950. John Luther Long (1861–1927), who wrote the story that became

Beth Sholom Synagogue was the only such sanctuary ever designed by the legendary architect Frank Lloyd Wright. Meaning the "House of Peace," Wright completed in 1959 the architectural marvel that symbolizes "the great mountain which Moses climbed to receive the Ten Commandments from God." *Kristopher Scott.*

Once standing on the south side of Church Road near High School Road, the home of Cheltenham's co-founder Toby Leech and his wife Hester was built on six hundred acres via a William Penn grant not long after Leech and his family arrived from England in 1682, according to the Old York Road Historical Society. Although crackers were baked on the premises during the Revolutionary War, Leech made a good living—with the help of slaves—by setting up a tanning yard, gristmill and baker's oven for sea biscuits. The home, badly burned about 1700, was renovated, according to the society. However, it was eventually razed during the early 1920s. *Courtesy of Jack and Mary Washington.*

the centerpiece of Puccini's *Madama Butterfly*, reportedly lived in the 200 block of Ashbourne Road. In 1983, the mega entertainer and educator, Dr. William "Bill" Cosby, took up residence on New Second Street (near Church Road) when he purchased a sprawling 4.5-acre property previously owned by Fitz Eugene Dixon Jr., the son of Fitz Eugene Dixon Sr., who had married Eleanor Widener Jr. (daughter of the George Dunton Widener who died on the *Titanic*). The property likely has roots to an original land grant dated September 10, 1683, regarding 250 acres belonging to John Ashmead, father-in-law of Cheltenham's co-founder Toby Leech.

Nearby, the granddaughter of William Elkins, Stella Elkins Tyler, who had married banker George F. Tyler, donated the mansion (on LaMott's perimeter) that she received as a wedding present to Temple University in 1935 for its art school, which recently relocated to the school's main campus in Philadelphia. Graduating from the Tyler School of Fine Arts was the likes of artist Simmie Knox, an African American painter chosen to paint the official White House portrait of former President Bill Clinton and First Lady Hillary Rodham Clinton.

Guineatown, Edge Hill and Glenside

Although this western area of the township was settled by wealthy Quakers such as Richard Morrey and his father Humphrey, who was the first mayor of Philadelphia (circa 1691), the black settlement called Guineatown developed following Richard's relationship with a house slave, Cremona. After bearing five children and following the death of Richard, who bequeathed Cremona Morrey two hundred acres of land, she remarried a free black named John Fry. Richard had made earlier provisions to free Cremona and her children, one of the earliest examples of a white so-called master granting emancipation in America. Cremona Jr., one of Richard and Cremona's five children, later married a free black, John Montier, likely from Haiti or a Caribbean island with French influences. By the late 1700s, they had constructed a stone dwelling that still stands on Limekiln Pike several blocks below what is today Arcadia University. During the colonial era, at least a dozen black families or more settled nearby, creating the settlement of Guineatown with an adjacent cemetery. During the Revolutionary War era, General George Washington's troops faced off with the British in the area in what became known as the Battle of Edgehill, the name that had evolved for the community likely due to the rolling hills in the vicinity. The area during the 1800s also became a settlement for Italian Americans, attracted by work at local quarries. The community eventually became known as Glenside, developed by William Taylor Blake Roberts, the developer of Latham and Ogontz Parks. After the Civil War, the sugar magnate, William Harrison, settled in the area on a huge estate, contracting the famed architect Horace Trumbauer to build "The Towers," a general replica of an ancient English castle (Alnwick). After this came the subdivision of his land, as the 1900s ensued and following Harrison's death in 1927.

The proud congregation of the LaMott African Methodist Episcopal Church poses for a Sunday picture. Many in the circa 1940–50 image undoubtedly had ancestral ties to

such early black families as the Tripletts and Bowsers. *Norman Triplett and the Old York Road Historical Society.*

CHELTEN HILLS, CAMPTOWN AND LAMOTT: INTEGRATION TRIUMPHS AND CIVIL RIGHTS

Initially known as Chelten Hills and then Camptown, the LaMott Historic District "is an unusual example of a racially integrated 19th-century community," according to Beth Savage's 1994 book *African American Historic Places*, sponsored by the National Register of Historic Places; the area was placed on the register in 1985. Situated on a portion of the site of the country's first and largest Federal training camp for African American troops during the Civil War, the community of LaMott was developed with the active participation of African Americans, as well as an influx of Irish immigrants and modern natives of Korea.

In fact, historical records and several online sources indicate that William C. Butcher was the first black resident of LaMott. The Virginia native was hired as a tenant farmer by Edward Davis for Oak Farm. Butcher's home was constructed at the corner of what is today Willow and Butcher Streets, obviously named for the Butcher family. Other blacks worked in the area, too, often for the wealthy tycoons who sometimes contributed money for some of the early black institutions in the area. Such first-generation black landowners as the Bowsers and Tripletts, who still live in the area today, attended the LaMott African Methodist Episcopal Church, built in 1888 on land donated by Davis. Infrastructure improvements—including utilities, streetlights and even police patrols—were in part funded by George Widener Sr.

Savage points out that the "community represents the transformation of the social and racial development of residential enclaves in the post–Civil War era," led by the likes of the black resident William A. Ritchie, the butler of the nearby Elkins estate. In addition to purchasing several properties, Ritchie "organized the Fairview Cemetery Company in 1907, serving as its first president." A decade later he helped to create the LaMott Building and Loan Association, "which helped more than 20 black families purchase homes and assisted in the establishment of four black-owned businesses."

Still, there were other major black contributors to the community. "In addition to Ritchie, William Anderson and Aubrey Bowser were locally noted civic leaders," Savage noted. "In 1915 Anderson became the first black policeman in Cheltenham. Aubrey Bowser, a descendant of William Bowser, one of LaMott's earliest black landowners, became a judge, achieving national prominence as one of the original members of the National Association for the Advancement of Colored People." He contributed and helped to found the NAACP's *Crisis* magazine, edited by the great black scholar W.E.B. Du Bois. Born in 1886, Bowser was also one of the first African Americans to graduate from Harvard University, as well as the first black graduate from Cheltenham public schools in 1907 to attend the institution.

Of further note, Bowser was also a noted writer with film experience and a teacher in New York City, as well as the son-in-law of one of the leading black journalists of the nineteenth century, T. Thomas Fortune, editor of the *New York Age*, for whom Bowser worked. A short story, "The Man Who Would Be White," written by Bowser, was adapted into a film screenplay. Along with Paul Laurence Dunbar and Wallace Johnson, Aubrey Bowser was one of seven authors who contributed to making films focusing on black culture via the renowned Reol films that became very significant in emphasizing the incredible talent pool of the Harlem Renaissance. Bowser also wrote for the *National Review* magazine.

The Triplett family of LaMott also made many noteworthy accomplishments, including Wallace Triplett, the first African American to be drafted in the National Football League. Triplett, the fifth of six sons born to Mahlon and Estella Triplett, played for the Detroit Lions as a running back and return specialist from 1949 to 1950. His portrait hangs in Canton, Ohio, in the Football Hall of Fame. Becoming the first National Football League player to be drafted in to the armed forces for the Korean War, Triplett after active duty was traded to the Chicago Cardinals before retiring from professional football in 1953.

In 1999, Triplett was inducted into the Cheltenham High School Hall of Fame, which noted that he "has been called the 'Jackie Robinson of Penn State football,' a pioneer in the civil rights struggle." Graduating from the high school in 1945, he "was the first African-American ever to start and the first to earn a varsity letter on a Penn State football team," too often facing Jim Crow racism, especially by other teams and townsfolk while on the road.

Furthermore, "Wallace Triplett wrote a carefully-researched history of LaMott in 1949," Elaine Rothschild noted in her 1991 *Old York Road Historical Society Bulletin* article "Historic LaMott." His brother, the late historian Perry Triplett, was inducted into the Cheltenham High School Hall of Fame in 1993 for his "tireless fight to create the LaMott National Historical Landmark," according to the school's inductee data. He formed the Citizens for the Restoration of Historical LaMott (CROHL) during the 1960s, which today continues to fulfill his great mission to preserve the neighborhood and recognize Camp William Penn and its warriors, as well as Lucretia Mott and associated antislavery abolitionists.

Soon after the group started its work, Triplett—who published in 2001 a Dorrance-Publishing pamphlet-book ("Martin: The Necktie, the Shirt, and the Wound") concerning the assassination of Reverend Dr. Martin Luther King, Jr.—"filed the necessary documents to have LaMott listed as a state historic district," Rothschild noted. "Finally, in 1974, Cheltenham Township passed an ordinance under Act 167" approving that status.

By 1987, CROHL "signed an agreement with the National Park Service to study the feasibility of designating a portion of LaMott as part of the National Park system," proposing "a visitor's center, a museum for black history, and a Lucretia Mott memorial garden, as possible tourist attractions and research facilities." Ultimately, though, the National Park Service "did not find LaMott suitable for inclusion in its system," partially based on the lack of physical evidence, despite CROHL refurbishing the camp's original front gates. Material from Camp William Penn, including wood, was said to have been used to construct neighborhood homes.

Actually, Camptown was acknowledged on the National Register as an important historic district because architecturally it is a very good example of post–Civil War residential development, as well as one of the first integrated residential communities in the nation, according to Rothschild. "The benefit the residents receive from this listing, besides prestige and recognition, is eligibility for tax rehabilitation benefits. However, since they also live in a state historic district under a local ordinance, they must obtain approval from the Cheltenham Township Board of Historical Architectural Review (BHAR) for any structural additions, alterations, or demolitions."

Meanwhile, CROHL recently funded and sponsored a popular documentary film about that first and largest federal training camp for black soldiers during the Civil War, as well as hosted book signings and other events pertaining to the facility. The group has shown artifacts and related material at area museums while it renovates an original LaMott firehouse, founded in 1910, to house the items.

Over the years, local historian Dr. James Paradis, a CROHL board member, has prolifically written about Camp William Penn, including in the book *Strike the Blow for Freedom*, concerning its revered Sixth Regiment USCT, whose members earned the Medal of Honor for combat at the Battle of New Market Heights in Virginia. Furthermore, the superb scholarship of

The LaMott fire station, established on Willow Avenue in 1910, is being renovated by a community group, Citizens for the Historic Restoration of LaMott, as a museum dedicated to Camp William Penn. It is now based near the southwest corner of Penrose Avenue and Humphrey Merry Way. *Old York Road Historical Society.*

Dr. James Elton Johnson, who wrote an extensive University of Pennsylvania doctoral thesis on Camp William Penn, has been invaluable for researchers and those interested in the camp's history.

Indeed, an excellent website, "Historic La Mott, Pennsylvania," developed by LaMott historian Bill Chambrés, contains an extraordinary amount of data, including articles, images, soldiers' rosters and so much more about the community and its famous Civil War training camp. The website can currently be found at www.historic-lamott-pa.com.

Sadly, Lucretia Mott's Roadside was demolished in 1912, the year that George and Harry Widener (father and son) died on the *Titanic*, for the twenty-eight-acre Latham Park development built the same year. William T.B. Roberts, the primary developer, consolidated the Lucretia Mott property and the William L. Elkins estate, naming the section after Lewis Latham, an Elkins ancestor who had links to royalty in England. Roberts, who lived in a grand home on the southeast corner of Old York Road and Elkins Avenue,

Although Lucretia Mott's Roadside home was demolished to make way for the exclusive housing development Latham Park, this state marker is situated near the site of where her residence once stood. *Donald Scott Jr.*

initiated a thorough marketing campaign by printing a brochure that detailed the area's physical beauty and noted its affluent residents. Roberts was also responsible for developing other areas of the township, often with the help of Trumbauer. After Roberts's 1936 death, his home was demolished by 1962 when the Greek Orthodox Church of the Annunciation bought the site.

Today, a state historic marker stands in front of the main gates of Latham Park on Old York Road several blocks above what is today Cheltenham Avenue and not far from the Greek church that indicates the location where Roadside once stood and its magnificent historic significance.

PART V

LEGACY OF CIVIL RIGHTS

Dr. Martin Luther King Jr.'s Speeches at Salem Baptist Church and Cheltenham High School

The tremendous early freedom fighters associated with LaMott portended future civil rights icons and African American trailblazers who made significant visits or eventually resided in the township.

For instance, during the 1960s the Reverend Dr. Martin Luther King Jr. visited the area on several occasions and spoke to standing room–only audiences in nearby Jenkintown Borough at Salem Baptist Church and Cheltenham High School in Wyncote.

As an alumnus of Morehouse College in Atlanta, Georgia, with the pastor of Salem Baptist Church of nearby Jenkintown—the Reverend Dr. Robert Johnson Smith Sr.—King accepted an invitation and gave two rousing sermons regarding civil rights during the mid-1960s. Crowds were so dense that Jenkintown streets had to be blocked off as hordes of people filled the sanctuary and gathered in front of the church.

King was also the featured speaker at an adult school lecture series (1963–64) sponsored by Cheltenham High School's adult division after he delivered in 1963 perhaps the greatest speech of his short lifetime, "I Have a Dream." He spoke at Cheltenham High on Wednesday, April 15, 1964. His lecture about race relations is still remembered by former students who were fortunate enough to witness those incredible moments in history. King was assassinated at age thirty-nine in 1968.

In fact, entertainers Felix Justice and Danny Glover presented "An Evening with Martin and Langston" several years ago during the Five Star Forum (lecture series) that focused on the principles and lives of the great African American writer Langston Hughes and Dr. King. Justice—who directed Glover in the South African play *The Blood Knot* and was known for his one-man presentation *Prophecy in America*—brought to life the words of King while Glover theatrically read many of Hughes's outstanding works.

Glover, the star of many blockbuster films such as *Lethal Weapon*, *The Color Purple*, *Dreamgirls* and *Beloved*, has been a prolific social activist who has garnered many noteworthy acting recognitions, as well as the NAACP's coveted Image Award.

Over its history of more than a half-century, the forum has presented blockbuster speakers ranging from great academic intellectuals to social philosophers and mathematical theorists.

In recent years, Cheltenham has become home to such momentous black social activists as Bobby Seale, former chairman of the Black Panther Party for Self Defense; Dr. Leonard Barrett, who marched in 1965 with King in Alabama during "Bloody Sunday" on March 7 and is now a retired Temple University professor who authored the landmark book *The Rastafarians*; and Dr. Molefi Kete Asante, the founder of the first doctoral program in black studies and developer of the Afro-centric concept. Asante, a renowned Temple University professor, has written more than seventy books pertaining to African and African American studies. The educator and entertainer Dr. Bill Cosby, an Elkins Park resident, has been at the forefront of addressing equality issues while urging African Americans to be more self-critical, sometimes causing controversy.

Today, Cheltenham's branch of the NAACP, along with other community groups over the years, has been concerned about equality in education, the workplace and real estate; the group has monitored and pushed for equitable hiring and testing for recruits interested in joining the Cheltenham police force and in other nearby municipalities. The group has also addressed other areas of equal opportunity and civil rights.

Matters have come full circle since the early 1900s and the days when Aubrey Bowser, the African American scholar, journalist and writer, became an original member of the NAACP and wrote for its crusading magazine *Crisis*, founded by the great W.E.B. Du Bois.

PART VI

FIGHTING FIRE AND CRIME

Firing Up History

Perhaps there were no other groups of people risking more to maintain the safety of Cheltenham than those in the fire and police departments, important centerpieces of the township. Such organizations were often the heart of the community, according to the following information gathered from the Old York Road Historical Society and Cheltenham's public information.

One of the earliest firefighting groups was the Cheltenham Hook and Ladder Company No. 1, which was started in September 1896 and located on the 500 block of Ryers Avenue. The building was expanded in 1906 before the company moved to the 400 block of Ryers Avenue about 1923. The building today serves as a business office. Over the years, the company's volunteer force has combated many infernos and saved the lives of residents and their properties.

Slightly older than Cheltenham Hook and Ladder is the Ogontz Fire Company, which was organized in 1892. Although the group's truck was initially stored in the township's garage, the company by 1925 relocated to the 8000 block of Old York Road and was headquartered there until May 1953. Today, the company is located in the 8200 block of Old York Road, fighting such late 1900s ferocious fires at the historic Breyer property

The LaMott Fire Company in this image is being served what appears to be coffee and donuts by the Second Alarmers Company in this March 1946 image. *Old York Road Historical Society.*

when the surviving building of the estate, Oak Lodge, was destroyed. The building, once part of the John Wanamaker estate, had been used by the Boy Scouts of America. Ogontz also responded to the flames that destroyed the one-hundred-year-old building that housed the Yorktown Inn, a mainstay of the community, in 1989. All of the township fire companies reportedly responded to that fire.

The LaMott Fire Company was founded on August 18, 1910, as a volunteer fire protection club ultimately called the LaMott Fire Association. The name was changed to LaMott Fire Company No. 1 when it was incorporated in May 1911. In 1914, the fire company moved to new quarters at 1618 Willow Avenue. The location was again switched on October 6, 1980, to the southwest corner of Penrose Avenue and Humphrey Merry Way. Situated near Philadelphia's border and covering the sprawling Lynnewood Gardens apartment complex, the company is poised to respond to a variety of emergencies.

Likely a subsidiary of the massive Lehigh Coal and Navigation Company, organized in 1818, the Philadelphia Lehigh Coal Company operated out of Elkins Park at least through 1951. The conglomerate was operational until the early 1960s. *Old York Road Historical Society.*

Meanwhile, the Oak Lane Terrace Improvement Association was organized near the city border in Cheltenham, north of Cheltenham Avenue on Crest Avenue. The group was needed due to the area's very rapid growth despite being disbanded about 1918. However, the original headquarters still exists, despite modifications over the many years.

Organized in 1900, the Glenside Fire Company's first firehouse was located at Glenside and Lismore Avenues. In 1927, the company moved to a new building just one hundred yards from the old location. A one-story addition to that building was completed in 1949. In 1924, it started officially training volunteer firemen, a trend that other stations followed nationally during the ensuing years. Its territory is filled with historic homes, residential neighborhoods and businesses reliant on the bravery and services of the Glenside Fire Company.

The Elkins Park Fire Company, originally known as the Old York Road Fire Company of Cheltenham, obtained the first motorized pumper in Cheltenham Township in 1913 and an additional sophisticated pump via a 1925 gift from the transportation magnate Peter A.B. Widener, patriarch of the family. That pumper, in fact, earned the "Best in the East" award at the 1926 Sesquicentennial Exhibition in Philadelphia. Meanwhile, more than a half-century later, educator and entertainer Bill Cosby donated an industrial gas range to the company's kitchen in 1983. Over the years, Elkins

Park has fought a number of fires with updated equipment, including the Coventry Dinner Theatre fire on New Year's Eve Day in 1974 and the Philadelphia Lehigh Fuel Company Coal Yard inferno in the 7800 block of Montgomery Avenue. In 1994, every township fire company, including Elkins Park, responded to a fire at Beth Jacob Building (a Jewish school), previously known as the Old Cheltenham High School, at Montgomery Avenue and High School Road.

Indeed, every one of the five volunteer departments in the township has responded to life- and property-threatening fires throughout their histories, always willing to join forces when necessary but proudly retaining their historic identities.

POLICE: FROM HORSE PATROLS TO SQUAD CARS

Wherever there has been substantial development, including in Cheltenham, some matters could only be handled by an effective police department.

Organized in February 1903 just after Cheltenham became a first-class township in 1900, the department initially operated in township offices located on Church Road, east of Old York Road. However, by 1957, operations were based at the former Breyer estate, where the primary township building is also located.

The first person to become chief of the organization—according to the department's history that can be accessed via the township and a website maintained by Bill Chambres (the historian laureate of the township)—was John Saddington for a two-year appointment at a monthly salary of seventy-five dollars. He asked for funding to hire seven mounted officers to patrol seven districts. An eighth district, Lynnewood Gardens, was added in 1973.

By May 1903, the first commendation of the department went to Officer William Goering for saving lives during a fire in the Oak Lane section of the township. There were several other interesting developments and recognitions for bravery during those early years, according to the department's online history.

Early technology advances were made in 1905 when Chief Saddington was given permission to establish a wire to his home so that he could receive notice at any hour concerning problems in the township. And by 1906, with township officials obviously pleased with Saddington's job performance, he was

Dedicated crossing guards in Cheltenham pose in front of what is today the township's administration building, once the grand mansion of the Henry W. Breyer estate, who expanded and directed a huge ice cream kingdom. The Cheltenham Police Department, organized February 1903, today is also based on the premises. *Old York Road Historical Society.*

appointed for two more years, instituting comprehensive speed enforcement for an increasingly popular contraption on township roads—automobiles, or horseless buggies. Fines were said to be exceptionally severe, depending on the situation, ranging from $10 to even $100.

However, by 1907, following friction with one of his officers and local officials, Saddington resigned from his job, not long after followed the five-year tenure of Chief Robert Lindsay, who modernized the department with call boxes established at various township locations and even replacing a couple of lame patrol horses.

Nonetheless, by 1914 Chief Gideon Lever was at the helm and improved investigative equipment, as well as acquired practical items, including raincoats. Historical sources indicate that he gained some notoriety in 1915 for being the first officer in the state to get a criminal conviction on a perpetrator via fingerprinting. Further, the first black police officer, William Anderson, was hired in 1915. Chief Lever then moved on to mechanizing the police department with motorized vehicles, despite leaving the department under pressure and amid controversy over his firing of an officer.

Since those early days, the Cheltenham Police Department has dealt effectively with crimes ranging from simple theft to murder, developing meanwhile into a sophisticated force of dozens of officers, including a SWAT (Special Weapons and Tactics) team with state-of-the-art communications equipment, as well as a detective division that has a forensic science unit with latent fingerprint expertise, a legacy of Chief Lever.

PART VII

LEGACY OF EDUCATION

Historical Overview

It's not surprising that education in Cheltenham has its roots to the original Quaker settlers of the area about three hundred years ago when on April 5, 1697, John Barnes deeded land to the Cheltenham Friends of the Dublin Meeting "for and toward the erection of a Meeting House for Friends and toward the maintenance of a school."

Indeed, the very early history of the township's schools is tied to the founding of the Abington Friends School in nearby Abington Township. Not more than a year after Barnes's appropriation, "the Cheltenham Friends asked the Philadelphia Quarterly Meeting for financial assistance to carry out the provisions of Barnes's deed," according to the research and writing of Alexander W. Scott, former principal of Cheltenham Elementary School and ex-president of the Old York Road Historical Society.

Actually, "by 1702 the Abington Friends School had opened its doors to children of the area," wrote Scott in his 1980 article "A History of Education in Cheltenham Township" for the *Old York Road Historical Society Bulletin.* "Since the majority of our early settlers were Quakers, the Abington Friends School remained the only school for the children of the Cheltenham area for over forty years."

Students of the Wyncote Elementary School during the early to mid-1900s are costumed in the attire of Cheltenham's colonial founders, including wigs and bonnets. Opened September 2, 1895, the building was located at the southwest corner of Greenwood Avenue and Walt Lane, remaining open until 1948. The Wyncote school is today located at Rices Mill and Church Roads. *Old York Road Historical Society.*

As the 1700s progressed, Cheltenham's increasing population required children to attend schools in what is today northwest Philadelphia. The students at those nearby schools hailed from such communities as Bristol (now Oak Lane), Germantown and Springfield Township, according to Scott.

However, by 1795, as some of the participating communities built their own schools, Cheltenham opened the Milltown School, the "real beginning of the Cheltenham School system," noted Scott. "This school must be considered one of the first schools, if not the first, in Montgomery County built as a public school with no religious affiliation." Students and their families, though, were required to pay tuition, amounting to several cents per day, as well as one dollar for books and other materials. The children of families who could not afford the costs were admitted free.

The township's first instructor, Samuel B. Wylie, hailed from Ireland and was educated at the University of Glasgow. He arrived in America on October 18, 1797, in New Castle, Delaware, making his way to Cheltenham and landing a job to teach at the Milltown School, according to Scott. Wylie must have been a brilliant man, by most accounts. In fact, by 1803, he was ordained and became the Presbyterian pastor of the First Reformed Church of Philadelphia. Always studious, Wylie in 1816 received a doctorate in divinity from Dickinson College. Then he served as principal for years at the University of Pennsylvania Academy and in 1828 became professor of ancient languages at the University of Pennsylvania. Wylie reportedly spoke fourteen different languages. Further, by 1834, he began serving as vice-provost of the university, retiring in 1848.

When a second room was added to the one-room schoolhouse in 1857, the school's name was changed to the Cheltenham School, a label that has characterized the district to this day. Then, by 1883, the building was demolished, with a new facility erected in the 400 block of Ashbourne Road and named the George K. Heller School, after a long-serving school official. The Heller School eventually became home to the Cheltenham Art Center after Cheltenham Elementary School opened in 1953.

As the various communities throughout the district developed over the years, elementary and middle schools were established, some becoming extinct depending on demographic trends. Yet several of the most important highlights, according to Scott's research, include the following.

The Harmer Hill School was built on Church Road near Rices Mill Road following an indenture dated March 24, 1842. Students living in the Edge Hill and Chelten Hills areas in the township's western end needed accommodations. By 1853, due to a shift in population growth within the township, a one-room schoolhouse was built "farther west on Church Road just past Limekiln Pike." The school at various times was referred to as Audenried, Harmer Hill and the Cheltenham Valley School.

Since the eastern and western ends of Cheltenham were covered by the Harmer and Milltown schools, students living in the middle of the township needed a school in their vicinity. The centrally located "Middle School" was ultimately established near Church Road on Mill Road with the deed dated November 14, 1859, not long before the Civil War would erupt in 1861. The name of the school was ultimately called the Shoemakertown School and then the Shoemaker School in tribute to Robert Shoemaker, a longtime school director.

With the decade between 1850 and 1860 showing in Cheltenham "the second greatest percentage increase" in population due to the development of the local railways, jumping "50 percent with the 1860 census showing 1,979 inhabitants," the district's schools proliferated. "In the years between 1860 and 1900 Cheltenham was to grow from 1,979 to 6,154 inhabitants and five more school buildings were to be erected."

Following the Civil War, Lucretia Mott's son-in-law Edward M. Davis built a school for the children of new homeowners in the La Mott area. A teacher was hired, and the school opened on February 3, 1868, with authorities renting the building for $7.50 a month. The school was ultimately purchased in August 1870 for $1,400 after extensive negotiations with Davis. "Due to the increased growth of the La Mott community a new school was opened at Willow and Sycamore avenues in November 1879 and continued there until its closing in 1940. The building still serves the community as the La Mott Community Center," wrote Scott.

Meanwhile, a high school was started during the 1880s after George W. Flounders, a principal of the Ashbourne School, made the suggestion to the school board. Ashbourne was built and opened in 1880 following the purchase of two lots on Union Avenue. That purchase was perhaps "the most important in the educational development of Cheltenham Township," according to Scott, keeping in mind that up to that point "all township schools in Pennsylvania, consisted of grades 1-9." Some "eleven years before the state was to pass a law establishing township high schools," according to Scott, "Cheltenham became one of the first, if not the first, township high school in Pennsylvania." The first four students graduated in June 1885 from Ashbourne.

In the Rowland Park area of Cheltenham, the Rowland School, named for the early entrepreneur Thomas Rowland, was opened in 1915 on Myrtle Avenue, according to the Old York Road Historical Society. Originally the structure was just four rooms. However, by 1924 the structure was increased to six rooms, with even more sections added in 1964 before the school closed in 1977 due to an enrollment drop. Today, the structure houses the East Cheltenham Free Library and the Rowland Community Center.

As the major wars occurred over the decades, affecting the economy and population trends, a number of schools throughout the township were closed, sometimes renamed, relocated and rebuilt as families moved into the township drawn by the excellent reputation of the educational system—explosive growth occurred during the 1950s and by 1960 hit almost 6,500 for district enrollment. Overall population was also skyrocketing.

The Lynnewood Elementary School opened its doors on February 25, 1952, at Washington Lane and Ashbourne Road, where the current school administration building is located and where the Cheltenham Military Academy started almost one hundred years earlier. Enrolled were future renowned poet Ezra Pound and President Ulysses Grant's son, Jesse. As the 1900s progressed, Pound lived much of his life in Europe associating with the likes of Gertrude Stein, Ernest Hemingway and Pablo Picasso. Yet his perceived anti-American

Cadets at the Cheltenham Military Academy included Ezra Pound (center with glasses), destined to become one of the world's greatest poets. It's hard to tell from this image that he'd also become one of the most rebellious. *Old York Road Historical Society.*

views led to his imprisonment once he returned to the states. He was eventually committed to St. Elizabeth's Mental Hospital in Washington, D.C., before being freed, dying in Italy in 1972 as a semi-recluse. A high school archaeology class commenced a four-year project to unearth a variety of artifacts after ruins were discovered in 1972 at the site of the old military school where Pound and Jesse Grant spent some formative time.

Other elite private schools would get started or flourish in Cheltenham, including the Ogontz School for Girls, an institute at which the famous female flier Amelia Earhart would get her schooling. Although the school had its origins in 1850 as the "Chestnut Street Female Seminary," in September 1883 arrangements "were made with Jay Cooke to rent his palatial home, at a cost of $15,000 per year," according to Suzanne Hilton's 1992 article "The Molding of a Young Lady at Ogontz School" in the *Old York Road Historical Society Bulletin*. That was after Cooke departed the residence to live with his daughter and son-in-law, Charles Barney, co-founder of the venerable financial services firm, Smith Barney Co.

The school's name was then changed to the Ogontz School for Young Ladies. Cooke, however, paid for extensive renovations and from time to time would sneak cookies and candy under his flowing cape to the girls, commodities

Cheltenham High School girls at the old facility practice Red Cross techniques in 1942 as World War II raged. Many of their classmates served in the war, as well as future township residents, including the late Arnold Snyder, who earned several Purple Hearts, a Bronze Star and a Silver Star for heroism at the Battle of the Bulge and Normandy's Omaha Beach. Memorials in Tookany Park and Curtis Arboretum, as well as veterans' lodges, pay homage to such warriors who have fought in virtually every American conflict or war since the country was founded. *Old York Road Historical Society.*

officially forbidden on campus. One graduate called Cooke "the dearest, most delightful, perennial Santa Clause any boarding school was ever lucky enough to have," according to Hilton. By October 1916, Amelia Earhart began studying at Ogontz, described as precocious and not afraid to speak her mind. Coming from a somewhat humble background in Kansas, she seemed to despise the haughtiness of some of her classmates, even occasionally bumping heads with the school's headmistress, Abby Sutherland. It was clear that the young lady would soon become a trailblazer. That same year, 1916, Sutherland, who managed to purchase the property from Cooke, began to search for another school site, which she found in nearby Abington. The school survived for decades at its new location in Rydal, but the property and all of its facilities were passed on to Penn State by Sutherland in 1950.

As the post–World War II baby boom would make a dramatic impact on the district, a modern high school, Cheltenham High School, and athletic fields were constructed in September 1959 near Rices Mill Road in Wyncote. Cedarbrook Middle School nearby was constructed in 1970. Over the years, both schools have received top recognition for superb academic programs, despite challenges that virtually all school districts face concerning funding, taxes and difficulties in curriculum development, especially as the township's population has become much more diverse.

The incredible accomplishments of Cheltenham High School's Hall of Fame inductees are an indication of the past greatness of the school system and its bright promise for the future. Perhaps the best way to gauge the health and potential of a community is to evaluate the success of its students and citizens and their impact on the world. Here are just a few of the graduates who've carried the legacy of the district and Cheltenham to exceptional heights, according to an associated Hall of Fame website for the school district.

Baseball Great Reginald "Reggie" Jackson

Reggie Jackson grew up in Wyncote, graduating from Cheltenham in 1964, and was inducted into the school's hall of fame in 1981. The four-sport varsity athlete, known as "Mr. October" for his outstanding play during World Series games, got his start on local fields and on the baseball team of the Greater Glenside Youth Club as the only black player. However, at the age of just thirteen, he was reputed to be the best ballplayer in town. Although his family life was challenging due to his parents' divorce, he had great respect for his father, who operated a dry-cleaning and tailoring shop on the first floor of the family residence. "Clean was the thing: Dad always demanded clean… Biggest sin in the world was to get the school clothes dirty. If I did, there was no discussion, nothing to argue about. If there were any problems with the clothes, there was always an excellent chance that Martinez Jackson would be looking to give a lickin," Jackson once told an interviewer. Throughout his professional career playing for Kansas City and Oakland A's, the California Angels and the New York Yankees, he had been voted to the American League All-Star team fourteen times. His hall of fame citation reads: "Reggie holds the major league career record for the most league championship series played (11), most games (45), most at-bats (163) and the American League records for most RBIs (20), most hits (37) and most singles (24)." Indeed Jackson's "Oakland teams won three consecutive World Series championships, the only organization other than the Yankees to three-peat, and his Yankee teams earned back-to-back titles in 1977–78." Ending his career in 1987, Jackson was voted to the American League All-Star team fourteen times before on August 1, 1993, being inducted into the Baseball Hall of Fame.

GRAMMY AWARD–WINNING JAZZ ARTIST MICHAEL BRECKER

Michael Brecker was inducted into the school's hall of fame in 1996, graduating during the height of the civil rights movement in 1967. Rated as one of the best tenor saxophone players of all time, Brecker was an eight-time Grammy winner noted for his "stylistic and harmonic innovations," according to his hall of fame biography, as well as "among the most studied instrumentalists in music schools throughout the world today." Music was a part of Brecker's life from the beginning. "Born into a musical household in 1949, Brecker's father played records" of many jazz greats. At Cheltenham Michael first studied the clarinet and alto sax before moving on to the tenor saxophone, his primary instrument. After leaving Indiana University during his first year and moving to New York City in 1970, he became part of a band at age twenty-one called Dreams, which included his brother Randy (inducted into Cheltenham High's Hall of Fame in 1963) and the great drummer Billy Cobham. Throughout his career, he would go on to work with the likes of Quincy Jones, Freddie Hubbard, Herbie Hancock, Chick Corea and many more. On January 13, 2007, Brecker died from complications of leukemia in New York City.

MICHAEL S. BROWN, MD, WINNER OF THE 1985 NOBEL PRIZE IN MEDICINE

Michael Brown graduated from Cheltenham High in 1958. He's renowned for "discoveries about cholesterol that could help prevent heart attacks and strokes." The molecular geneticist maintained a "life-long fascination with science," starting "with an amateur radio operating license obtained at the age of 13, while a student at Thomas Williams Junior High School in Wyncote," his biography says. He also nurtured his great interest in writing at Cheltenham High. Graduating from the University of Pennsylvania undergraduate school and School of Medicine, Brown was elected to the prestigious Phi Beta Kappa for academic excellence. During his distinguished career he has worked at the University of Texas Southwestern Medical School in Dallas and at the University of Texas and has written for many professional publications, as well as received a long list of awards. In his spare time, the 1987 Cheltenham Hall of Fame inductee is "an avid windsurfer," according to his biography.

JoAnne A. Epps: A Former Assistant U.S. Attorney, Law School Professor and Associate Dean

JoAnne Epps graduated from Cheltenham High in 1969 and was inducted into the hall of fame in 1999. She was quite aware of the climaxing civil rights movement as an African American woman living during the 1960s. Voted as homecoming queen and vice-president of the student body, she attended Trinity College in Hartford, Connecticut, and received a law degree from Yale University School of Law in 1976. Her hard work paid off when in 1976 Epps rose to the job of deputy city attorney for Los Angeles. She then became in 1980 the assistant U.S. attorney for the Eastern District of Pennsylvania. By 1985, she had joined the faculty of Temple University School of Law, soon to become the first woman to receive the George P. Williams III Memorial Award for "outstanding excellence in teaching." She has also served as the school's associate dean for academic affairs.

Israel Prime Minister Benjamin Netanyahu

Benjamin Netanyahu, a 1967 graduate of Cheltenham High, is today serving a second term as the primary leader of Israel. Originally born in Tel Aviv in 1949, he moved to the United States at age thirteen and in high school here "impressed teachers and fellow students with his academic brilliance and... strong convictions," according to his hall of fame biography that also notes his 1999 induction. Skipping graduation ceremonies, Netanyahu joined Israeli forces during the Six-Day War with Egypt, serving "five years as an officer in an elite paratrooper unit of the Israel Defense forces." He participated in many antiterrorist missions. After earning a bachelor's in architecture in 1974 and master's degree in management studies in 1976 from the Massachusetts Institute of Technology, he co-founded the Jonathan Institute dedicated to researching terrorism. The organization was named after his brother, Jonathan, who died during the 1976 mission to rescue hostages at Uganda's Entebbe Airport. Jonathan was a 1964 graduate of Cheltenham High and was inducted in 1984 into the school's hall of fame. Authoring articles and books about terrorism over the years, Netanyahu served as Israel's ambassador to the United Nations from 1984 to 1988 before ascending to a number of important political positions, soon gaining an important international profile as a fierce representative of Israel's causes. In March 1993, he was elected to the chairmanship of the Likud Party, becoming prime minister of Israel in 1996. Netanyahu's hard-line opposition against the Palestinians, though, led to his May 1999 defeat because many Israelis advocated for greater peace. In the recent 2009 elections, Netanyahu was the Likud's candidate for prime minister again, using Internet techniques that were strikingly similar to the newly elected American leader, President Barack Obama, the first African American to ascend to that post. Netanyahu consequently won his election, making him again one of the most influential and powerful leaders in the world.

LISE MARLOWE: NATIONAL HISTORY TEACHER OF THE YEAR

In recognition of Cheltenham's incredible history, Lise Marlowe, a Cheltenham native who attended local schools, won the coveted History Teacher of the Year award in 2006 from television's the History Channel, as well as a $5,000 grant, for prolifically focusing her Elkins Park Middle School sixth-grade students on the area's exceptional past. The effervescent young woman had guided her students to produce a sixty-five-minute film documentary, a fifty-page book and a mural concerning Camp William Penn and Lucretia Mott. During a three-day commemoration in Washington, D.C., she received a tour of the White House and the award from First Lady Laura Bush. And with the grant proceeds, her students will produce a Holocaust documentary by interviewing local Jewish survivors of that horrific event in world history. Quite appropriately, she's a fierce advocate of diversity and tolerance, attributes of many of Cheltenham's most historic figures.

BIBLIOGRAPHY

Bacon, Margaret Hope. *Valiant Friend: The Life of Lucretia Mott.* New York: Walker and Company, 1980.

Bean, Theodore W., ed. *History of Montgomery County Pennsylvania, Illustrated, 1884.* Philadelphia: Everts & Peck. http://usgwarchives.net/pa/montgomery/beantoc.htm.

Black, Edward, Jr. "History of the Police Department." Historic La Mott, Pennsylvania. Chambrés & Associates. www.historic-lamott-pa.com.

Brandon, William. *The American Heritage Book of Indians.* New York: Dell Publishing Co., Inc., 1961.

Chambres, William. Historic La Mott, Pennsylvania. Chambrés & Associates. www.historic-lamott-pa.com.

"Cheltenham High School Hall of Fame: Biographies." Cheltenham High School Alumni Association. http://cheltenhamalumni.org.

"Cheltenham: Stetson Hats—'The Hat of the West' is Born." Cheltenham Township. http://www.cheltenhamtownship.org.

"Cheltenham Township." Living Places by the Gombach Group. http://www.livingplaces.com.

Clemmer, Leon. "The Steeles of Caversham Mansion and Ballanreas, Cheltenham." *Old York Road Historical Society Bulletin* 44 (1984).

Didbin, Thomas Foghall. *The History of Cheltenham, and Accounts of its Environs.* Cheltenham, England: H. Ruff, 1803.

"Felt and Straw Stetson Hats History." Hat History. http://www.hathistory.org/stetson/index.html.

Finck, Lila. "The Legend of Ogontz." *Old York Road Historical Society* 44 (1984).

Foust, Doreen. "Wyncote's Historic District." *Old York Historical Society* 47 (1987).

Hilton, Suzanne, and Frank Devlin. "A Guide to the Stained Glass Windows of St. Paul's Episcopal Church." *Old York Road Historical Society Bulletin* 52 (1992).

Hilton, Suzanne. "The Molding of a Young Lady at Ogontz: From 100 Years of Ogontz, by Abby A. Sutherland." *Old York Road Historical Society Bulletin* 52 (1992).

"John Wanamaker." Pennsylvania Biographies. http://www.geocities.com/Heartland/4547/wanamaker.html.

Leach, Robert J. "The Hicksite Separation on Nantucket." *Quaker History, the Bulletin of Friends Historical Association* 71, no. 1 (1982).

Lippincott, Horace Mather. "Jay Cooke." *Old York Road Historical Society Bulletin* 10 (1946).

———. "Richard Wall and George Shoemaker." *Old York Road Historical Society Bulletin* 9 (1945).

———. "Toby Leach." *Old York Road Historical Society Bulletin* 11 (1947).

Marshall, Logan, ed. *The Sinking of the Titanic and Great Sea Disasters*. N.p.: The Vision Forum, Inc., 1998.

Morgan, Ralph. "Preserving the Heritage of Cheltenham Township." *Old York Road Historical Society Bulletin* 9 (1945).

Muhlenberg, Henry Melchior. *The Pennsylvania-German in the Revolutionary War*. N.p.: Clearfield Co., 1999.

Newport, David. "Jenkintown in 1834 and Hatboro in 1846." *Old York Historical Society Bulletin* 51 (1991).

New York Times. "After More Pittsburg Roads, Widener and Elkins said to be on a Purchasing Trip." May 7, 1892. Accessed via http://www.proquest.com.

———. "The Biggest Syndicate Yet." April 27, 1890. Accessed via http://www.proquest.com.

———. "Only Seeking the Earth." April 12, 1886. Accessed via http://www.proquest.com.

———. "Put in the Syndicate's Hands. Widener and His Friends Now Directors of the Seventh-Avenue Road." June 15, 1886. Accessed via http://www.proquest.com.

———. "Slaves of a Syndicate: Philadelphia Ruled by the Traction Company." April 7, 1886. Accessed via http://www.proquest.com.

———. "Widener and Company." May 24, 1886. Accessed via http://www.proquest.com.

———. "Widener, Elkins and Company." June 7, 1886. Accessed via http://www.proquest.com.

———. "Widener Takes the Trick: The Philadelphians Capture the Seventh-Avenue Road." June 7, 1886. Accessed via http://www.proquest.com.

———. "William L. Elkins Dead." November 8, 1903. Accessed via http://www.proquest.com.

———. "W.L. Elkins Very Ill." October 14, 1903. Accessed via http://www.proquest.com.

Old York Road Historical Society. *Images of America: Cheltenham Township*. Charleston, SC: Arcadia Publishing, 2001.

Pitts, Reginald H. "The Montier Family of Guineatown." *Old York Road Historical Society Bulletin* 53 (1993).

———."Moses Highgate, Miller of Cheltenham Township." *Old York Road Historical Society Bulletin* 49 (1989).

———. "Robert Lewis of Guineatown, and 'The Colored Cemetery in Glenside.'" *Old York Road Historical Society Bulletin* 51 (1991).

Platt, Frederick. "Horace Trumbauer in Jenkintown." *Old York Road Historical Society Bulletin* 44 (1984).

———. "Horace Trumbauer's Latest Works in Glenside." *Old York Road Historical Society Bulletin* 40 (1980).

———. "Horace Trumbauer's Other Works in Elkins Park." *Old York Road Historical Society Bulletin* 47 (1987).

Rothschild, Elaine W. "From Ashmeads to Bill Cosby." *Old York Road Historical Society Bulletin* 44 (1984).

———. *A History of Cheltenham Township.* Cheltenham Township, PA: Cheltenham Township Historical Commission, 1976.

Rothschild, Elaine W., and Suzanne McLean Hilton. "Historic Buildings on the National Register of Historic Sites in the Old York Road Area." *Old York Road Historical Society Bulletin* 39 (1979).

———. "Historic LaMott." *Old York Road Historical Society Bulletin* 51 (1991).

———. "The Man Behind Cheltenham's Curtis Arboretum." *Old York Road Historical Society Bulletin* 39 (1979).

Scott, Alexander W. "A History of Education in Cheltenham Township." *Old York Road Historical Society Bulletin* 40 (1980).

———. "Origin of the Rowlands of Cheltenham." *Old York Road Historical Society Bulletin* 39 (1979).

Scott, Donald, Sr. "Camp William Penn's Black Soldiers in Blue." *America's Civil War* (November 1999).

———. *Images of America: Camp William Penn*. Charleston, SC: Arcadia Publishing, 2008.

———. "Titanic Tragedy Shows Family's Heart & Soul." *Family History* magazine (May/June 2004).

"The Story of Grey Towers: A Great American Castle." Arcadia University. www.arcadia.edu/about/default.aspx?id=579.

Taylor, John C. "A Sketch of General Louis Wagner." *Old York Road Historical Society Bulletin* 9 (1945).

Time. "Art: Widener to Washington." October 28, 1940.

Wallace, Paul A.W. *Indians in Pennsylvania*. Harrisburg, PA: Commonwealth of Pennsylvania, the Pennsylvania and Museum Commission, 1981.

Whitemire, David. "The Wideners: An American Family." Encyclopedia Titanica. http://www.encyclopedia-titanica.org/widener-family.html.

Winch, Julie. *A Gentleman of Color: The Life of James Forten*. Oxford: Oxford University Press, 2002.